Katie
AND
Peter
Moving On

EMILY HERBERT

Katie
AND
Peter
Moving On

JB

JOHN BLAKE

Published by John Blake Publishing Ltd,
3 Bramber Court, 2 Bramber Road,
London W14 9PB, England

www.johnblakepublishing.co.uk

First published in paperback in 2010

ISBN: 978 1 84454 972 6

British Library Cataloguing-in-Publication Data:

A catalogue record for this book is available from the British Library.

Design by www.envydesign.co.uk

Printed in Great Britain by CPI Bookmarque, Croydon, CR0 4TD

3 5 7 9 10 8 6 4 2

Papers used by John Blake Publishing are natural, recyclable products made
from wood grown in sustainable forests. The manufacturing processes
conform to the environmental regulations of the country of origin.

CONTENTS

CHAPTER ONE
A WHIRLWIND WEDDING

The dust was beginning to settle: Katie Price and Alex Reid had been married for a month now, and the world was now starting to get used to the fact that a new Mr Katie Price was in town. The couple had had a whirlwind romance, followed by a surprise wedding, but it was increasingly clear that they were genuinely committed to one another. Clearly, the cynics who had said it was all a publicity stunt were in the wrong.

And yet the story continued to fascinate. Even though Katie had so very publicly remarried, the presence of Peter Andre, her first husband – who had left her less than a year previously, and from whom she had only recently been divorced – was still very much in evidence. Though he and Katie very rarely saw one another and that tended to be when they were handing over the children – Harvey, from Katie's relationship with the footballer Dwight Yorke, and Junior Savva Andreas and Princess Tiaamii Crystal Esther, their children together – even so, they were still very much perceived to be part of the same story in the public's eye. Whether or not he wanted it, Pete had found himself to be part of a triangle that continued to fascinate and everything he said or did still intrigued the public, much as it did when he was with Katie. His recent affair with the Page 3 girl Maddy Ford had generated an enormous amount of publicity and merely fuelled the public's desire to know more about everything that was going on in their lives.

Not that it did much to mend relations with Katie. Indeed, it merely appeared to add to the anger already felt by his ex-wife. 'Finally this news will show a side to Peter that has never come out before – no more Mr Nice Guy!' snapped Katie. 'This story just shows his true colours: he is not the perfect man like he claims to be – he's a liar. I have never deceived anyone. Nobody can knock the fact that I have been up front from the word go about my relationship with Alex; I made it clear the moment I was with someone else. All that time Peter has been on my back about what I have been getting up to with Alex, but he is no different.'

It was yet another bruising exchange that demonstrated quite how hostile towards one another the erstwhile couple remained. Even though it had only been a few years since Katie married Pete in a fairytale-themed wedding, complete with pink princess dress, a tiara and a glass coach, there was certainly no love lost between the two of them now. Anything and everything could become a bone of contention and frequently did: Pete had comprehensively turned against the woman he'd once loved, while Katie was still furious at his rejection of her, which meant that life was unlikely to settle down at any point yet.

And in the decade or so since she had come to the attention of the public, Katie had been loved and loathed, but never ignored, and the same appeared to apply to the men she got involved with, too. Katie tended to dominate her men – that had become one of the problems between herself and Pete – but the sheer force of her presence and personality meant that once in the limelight with her, that was where they tended to stay. In truth, Pete certainly didn't want to exit the public view – he had a career in music to promote, after all – but the price he had to pay was that the constant warfare between the two of them was not only almost permanent, but all too fascinating for anyone else to ignore.

But Katie was married again now: to Alex. Initially viewed by the public with some degree of suspicion, the cross-dressing cage fighter was beginning to win over Katie's fans. Recently, he had taken part in *Celebrity Big Brother*, emerged the winner and almost immediately afterwards he had wed Katie on 2 February in a low-key ceremony in Las Vegas. To spend any time in Katie's orbit it was essential to be able to respond to events as quickly as she did – and indeed, it was obvious that Alex was learning fast.

So fast, in fact, that it emerged that he was as surprised by the wedding plans as everyone else. It was while he'd been in the *Big Brother* household that Katie had plotted their next move – Alex himself only learnt about it very late on. Nor were his parents exactly thrilled. 'The wedding was whirlwind and a bit of a surprise,' he admitted. 'Katie planned it all. My mum and dad – my whole family, in fact – were a bit gutted. I managed to tell my mum in a quick call just minutes before, but no one else. I didn't get married for them, anyway. I got married for me – to make Alex Reid happy.'

They certainly appeared to be settling down nicely together, although Alex was very keen to clear up another misunderstanding: it had been reported that he had bought Katie a relatively cheap ring. That was not, however, the case. 'The stories saying that the ring I bought Katie only cost £2,200 caused me a lot of trouble,' he confessed. 'She hit the roof. I can't say how much I paid, but it's more like £60,000. You only get married once, don't you? And I wanted to push the boat out.'

Naturally, it had been a massive change in his life. Just a few months previously, no one had ever heard of Alex and now everyone in the country seemed to know exactly who he was. Opportunities that he might previously have only dreamed of were now opening up, although he also fully intended to enjoy married life. 'After this job I'm probably going to quit fighting for a bit,' he revealed on the eve of an upcoming fight. 'Work doesn't come first, Katie does. It's just been a mad few months – I've won *Big Brother* and got married to Katie Price. Mad!'

Indeed, the speed with which Katie was moving on was simply breathtaking. One of the secrets to her success, of course, was that she was rarely introspective and hardly ever looked back, but even so, to have put the relationship with Pete behind her so quickly and to married again so soon was staggering. And that was not all: Katie was already talking about an addition to the family, despite the fact that the two had only just wed. 'Me and Alex want kids and we're trying, so let's hope,' she confided. 'I can't wait to get pregnant.' It was clearly the start of a whole new life.

And it was a life that Katie was planning to be completely in control of. Shortly before a trip to Los Angeles to meet up with her new husband, she persuaded Alex to drop his manager of 12 years, Chris Herbert, and allow her to run his career instead. Apart from the fact that Katie liked to be in charge, matters appeared to have come to a head when Herbert arranged for his client to do a nude photoshoot for the cover of a gay magazine, which caused Katie to blow her top. 'Katie told Alex to let her run the show,' revealed a source. 'It's sad, they were good mates.' Perhaps so, but her own success was more than ample proof that Katie knew just what she was doing and so it was to prove.

There were, however, conflicting stories about the real reason why Katie forced Alex to pull out of the shoot. The magazine in question was *Attitude*: some insisted that Katie was livid that Alex wasn't being paid, while others said that she didn't want him to challenge her own popularity within the gay community by establishing his own following. Given that he did go on to do a nude cover shot, albeit for *Cosmopolitan* magazine, it would seem that the former was more likely, but the editor of *Attitude*, Matthew Todd, certainly hadn't been impressed by the episode. He later claimed Katie treated Alex, 'like a puppy on a lead,' and called her, 'the worst celebrity I have dealt with.'

The shoot, which had cost £5,000 to set up, had just got started when Katie arrived, recalled Todd. 'She turned up with a huge entourage two hours late and with no apology, when she wasn't even meant to be there,' he continued. 'She just turned into a monster. He just did as she said – he looked like a little dog on a lead with his tail between his legs.'

Nor was that all. Katie's great friend Gary Cockerill had accompanied her: a trained make-up artist, Katie insisted that he should be paid to work on Alex, despite the fact that alternative arrangements had already been made. But it was when she discovered that Alex was going to be naked that the trouble really began.

'She was screaming that it wouldn't be tasteful, which coming from her is unbelievable,' Todd continued. 'I've never had anyone screech like a loony in a shoot before. We have had amazing people like David Beckham and Robbie Williams, who all did shoots for us without any problems.'

While Katie could undoubtedly be difficult, however, this was overlooking the fact that she was also very good at what she did. She was a household name twice over, as Jordan and then Katie Price, and apart from a period when she seemed to go off the rails following the split with Pete, she had successfully transformed her image from a rather tawdry glamour girl constantly falling out of nightclubs into a very successful businesswoman and married mother of three. If ever there was a person who knew about the importance of image and how to put yourself across well, it was Katie, and no matter difficult she was being, clearly she still had an eye on what the future would hold.

As Katie increasingly took Alex in hand, some rather unkind rumours surfaced to the effect that she was trying to turn him into a second version of her ex. Alex was not amused: 'I can't believe people said she was trying to turn me into Pete,' he said. 'I don't think so! I don't look anything like him – I'm much more muscly for a start!' Indeed, the resemblance was not a striking one, but the fact was that Katie was taking a much more active role in his professional life, just as she had done with Pete, and there were noticeable differences in Alex's appearance. Altogether he was looking more polished than he had done previously and clearly that was something to do with his new wife. What's more, he already had his own reality television show about martial arts: *Alex Reid: The Fight of his Life*, due to be screened on Bravo in April 2010. The programme showed him travelling around the world to learn different types of martial arts while he prepared for his fight against the World Middleweight champ, Tom 'Kong' Watson.

Katie herself, meanwhile, was attracting more attention than ever. Landing in Los Angeles, she caused a near riot among waiting photographers as she passed through the airport: with stylist Gary Cockerill on one side and beautician Julie Williams on the other, she made her way through the crowd, dressed in grey leggings, grey fake fur jacket and shades. Her expression was inscrutable, although onlookers reckoned she would have been delighted with all the fuss. She was spotted spending the afternoon in a West Hollywood salon before dining at the fashionable Chateau Marmont with Gary. Both Katie and Alex continued to attract huge amounts of attention wherever they went, nor were they exactly shying away from it: the next day, Katie was filmed in full make-up having Botox injections – all for her reality television show.

She was certainly making the most of her time out in LA. Vinnie Jones, who had become friendly with Alex when they were both incarcerated in the Big Brother House, was now back in LA, where he was based: he threw a big dinner, to which Katie took Phil Turner, her friend and partner of her make-up artist

Gary Cockerill – Alex was still filming and couldn't be there. The two did manage to have lunch at The Ivy the next day, however, after which they visited Trashy Lingerie, an underwear emporium. Wags wondered if Alex, a self-confessed cross dresser, was actually the person the clothes were for.

But publicity of a less welcome kind greeted them now. The Las Vegas wedding had been so sudden and such a surprise that its details were still being raked over and there were now reports that the marriage might not actually be legal. The Revd. Mose Henney, the minister who married the couple, had been accused of bedding members of his congregation at a church in Wisconsin eight years previously and there were fears that his licence had been revoked. Three women had been involved and Henney, by now 67, had admitted, 'inappropriate sexual intercourse, with three adult women.' His signature, however, was clearly visible on Katie and Alex's wedding certificate, having married the pair at St Andrew's Lutheran Church.

When informed of the news, Alex became alarmed. 'You've got to be kidding!' he said. 'This is something I need to straighten out.' The situation was not, in fact, at all clear: 'Technically Jordan and Alex are not married,' said Steven Weinberg, a US lawyer. 'It is a very messy situation.' That was for sure.

Whatever the exact legal situation, though, Katie was adamant that she had finally met The One. However much she might have talked about moving on in the wake of the split with Pete, it was patently obvious that it had knocked her for six. In the immediate aftermath of his departure, Katie lost a huge amount of weight to become worrying thin and no matter how much she pressed on with her engagements, she was clearly in pain. Now, however, she was looking much happier – her whole demeanour was that of a woman at peace.

'Everything happens for a reason and I believe I was meant to be with Alex,' she declared. 'We get on fantastically; we have such a laugh together. And he's the fittest man I have ever, ever seen – he really is gorgeous. Plus it's fun, there's no hidden agenda. I am massively in love. With Alex I can be 100 per cent myself. He "gets" me and allows me to be who I am, and vice versa. I loved Pete, but with him, there were always issues.'

There certainly had been, and it was becoming increasingly apparent what those issues were. 'There was jealousy and I couldn't be out by myself without him on my back, demanding to know where I was or who I was with,' Katie continued. 'Alex doesn't ask where I am 24/7, he trusts me. And I trust him. We speak every day, and when we're not together we're still in contact, by text or phone or whatever. But what we have is private: it's special and I don't want it played out in public like Pete's and my marriage. This time I'm doing things differently. I love him so much and he loves me. I'd love for us to have kids. I want to be Reidinated more than anything! Trust me, we are trying. And when I try with Alex, I know about it! I thought I was pregnant earlier this week and went for tests at a Harley Street clinic, but they were negative. We're gutted.'

Katie really did seem to be happy at last. Meanwhile, yet another row with Pete had broken out, though. Katie was still smarting at the news of his affair: while there were many people who believed that at the bottom of it all she still loved her former husband and that was what really hurt, the lady herself was simply furious that he had put a great deal of emphasis on remaining celibate, when he was actually having a fling. In one of their uglier clashes the children got involved, however. Pete, of course, also had a reality show and the following, unedifying exchange took place: 'Tell your dad he is a liar!' Katie yelled, when Junior was on the phone to his father. 'Daddy's got a new girlfriend.'

'Do you have a new girlfriend, Daddy?' he asked, visibly upset. 'Mummy's telling me to yell at you.'

Pete was understandably livid himself: 'What a

terrible thing for a mother to do,' he said. 'Stop trying to pollute our children's minds – you're a terrible, terrible person!' He then told the camera: 'I am sick of her using our kids to wage her battles for her.'

Katie, however, had not got to where she was to let marital spats upset her. Still in LA, she had arranged for her visit to coincide with the Oscars and received an invitation to Sir Elton John's AIDS Foundation Academy Award Party, one of the most sought-after events of the season. Other guests included Kelly Brook, Heidi Klum, Christina Hendricks, Nicole Richie, Simon Cowell with his fiancée, Mezhgan Hussainy, Kelly and Sharon Osbourne, Jamie Foxx and other celebrities too numerous to mention.

One of those celebrities was, however, Victoria Beckham, with whom Katie had a history that went back quite a long way. The trouble began more than a decade earlier, when Victoria (allegedly) burst into a chorus of 'Who Let the Dogs Out?' when Katie entered the Manchester United hospitality area, where Victoria's husband David was then playing. Matters became worse a few years later when Victoria, attempting to launch a solo career, did some work with Dane Bowers – who just happened to be the boyfriend of one Katie Price. There is no suggestion whatsoever that anything improper happened between them, but it appeared that Dane admired

Victoria, something that did not improve the relationship with Katie, with whom he eventually split. But Katie got her own back: in 2004, when she entered the jungle in *I'm A Celebrity... Get Me Out Of Here!*, the occasion on which she met Pete, she hinted about secrets that she could reveal about David Beckham that were very sensational indeed. In the event, no such disclosures were made, but there was absolutely no love lost between the two women and they were called upon to negotiate the evening as skilfully as they could.

In fact, the Oscar party passed without incident. Victoria was looking her usual stylish self in one of her own gowns – a one-shouldered nude silk column – while Katie went for a more elegant choice than usual: a brilliant blue sequined number, backless, split to the thigh and with two large silk corsages. Her hair was twisted into a chignon and she sported large diamond studs in her ears. Katie had unsuccessfully attempted to engage Victoria in conversation at Elton's bash the previous year, perhaps feeling it was time to bury hatchets; this year, however, the two steered clear of one another and Victoria, having worked the crowd, went off to an exclusive event held by *Vanity Fair*.

There was, however, some serious strategic thinking going on behind the partying. Of course Katie wanted to hang out with some of the biggest movers and shakers in the entertainment world, but she wanted much more than that, too: she was eager to crack America. But it was a notoriously difficult market for British stars to make their way into, and so attending high-profile events such as this one was a way to become noticed, not least because it had helped other stars such as the Beckhams to find their way in.

'She won't get a foot in the door any other way,' revealed a source. 'This will be Jordan's fourth visit [to the States] in just over a year and each time she gets more exposure. She makes sure she keeps in with the gossip columnists like Perez Hilton – she sees no reason why she can't be just as big as the Beckhams have been, as she's going for a different market.' And now, of course, with Alex in tow it was two for the price of one – the perfect time to act.

Memories of her past as well as her future were still there, though. And curiously enough, the episode with Victoria Beckham was not the only aspect of Katie's former life to be resurrected in the early part of 2010. A couple of months previously, just before Katie and Alex got married, Dane Bowers emerged to reminisce about the past. Dane was to appear on *Celebrity Big Brother* with Alex and, mindful that it might be a little awkward to have her ex and current beau in the same house, Katie invited them both to a New Year's

Eve celebration, which had unfortunately ended in a row. By the time they reached the *Big Brother* house, however, peace had broken out and Dane was happy to explain that he and Katie had originally split up because of her propensity to undress. '[It was] lots of little things, really,' he told the house. 'If you hear her side of things it was because of Victoria – I was working too hard with Victoria – [but] at the time I was quite jealous. She stopped doing all the nudie shoots, the really naughty things. Then she did one just to spite me and I said, "If you do it, I'll leave you," and she did it. We were together two-and-a-half years – it was quite substantial, really.'

But the man that Katie had most recently shared her life with before Alex was still very much around. Sometimes it seemed as if not a day went by without another very public spat breaking out and the latest one centred round Pete taking the children to see him perform. In March, at the O2 Indigo, he did a very raunchy number with some of the dancers onstage, something that did not go down well with his ex missus, and Katie let rip.

'Peter is always having a go at her for keeping the kids up late and taking them to inappropriate things,' said a friend. 'But what could be more inappropriate than this? Letting your kids see you dance with a load of half-naked women is hardly in the parents' handbook! This is bound to be confusing for them and hardly something they should be going to.'

Pete, however, proved as impervious to criticism as his ex-wife. 'The kids were there and had a brilliant time,' his spokesperson commented. 'They took their pyjamas and changed into them before they left the Arena – they both loved it.'

Nor did he let it rest. 'Thanks to everyone who's been to the concerts the last couple of weeks,' he tweeted. 'You guys rock. Just finished indigo2 in London. Loved every min.'

Not that Katie was making matters easier herself and now she threatened to reveal to the world a side of Pete that no one else had ever seen. 'I don't want him to be unhappy, but people need to realise that he's not what the public think he is,' she explained earnestly. 'I want him to move on like I have, but he won't. You just wait! It's time the truth came out about me and Pete; I'm not going to hold anything back – I'd be very scared, if I was him.'

In actual fact, it was Katie who would shortly be made to eat her own words.

Pete was certainly keen to set the record straight as to what exactly he had (or had not) been doing. 'Kate claimed six months ago that I had a secret girlfriend and that the truth would come out one day,' he wrote in his magazine column in *New* magazine. 'A lot of people have therefore wrongly come to the conclusion that she was talking about Maddy [Ford]. I can categorically state that this is totally untrue and I have not had a girlfriend since my divorce. And, more to the point, I hadn't even met Maddy when Kate said this! I have never deliberately deceived anyone. I'm a single man. I said I'd remain celibate until after my divorce and I did.'

That, however, was not the end of it: Katie had been a little unwise in the manner in which she had been lashing out at her ex and it would shortly end up in court.

But Pete's distress over the continuing fallout from his fling was very real. He had made such an issue of remaining celibate after he and Katie split up that this was bound to cause a stir: apart from the fact that Katie was apparently milking the situation for all she was worth, he had been subjected to a fair amount of negative criticism in the press, too. In fact, he had done nothing wrong – the fling took place after his divorce when both he and Maddy were single and free to do as they wanted – but even so, it was clearly a source of angst that wouldn't go away.

Pete's birthday came round on 27 February but he didn't much feel like celebrating. 'To say Pete's birthday joy has fallen flat is an understatement,' observed a source. 'It's completely fizzled out. He feels betrayed by this girl. It is true that they had sex on a few occasions, but nothing more than that. Now it looks like she has sold her story and made much more of it than there was. The whole thing is like a hammer blow to Pete, coming just months after the heartbreak of splitting with Jordan, and, to add to that, a series of raunchy pictures of Maddy Ford have emerged. He was hoping to steer clear of the type of headlines his ex-wife has become known for. All taken together, this is not the sort of image Pete is hoping to project.'

Indeed, Pete was so upset about the whole thing that even his business manager, Claire Powell, was forced to speak up in his defence. 'Peter met this girl after his divorce came through and he has been intimate with her on a couple of occasions, but it was not serious,' she said. 'He always said he would make an announcement if he was in a serious relationship.'

His friends stood up for him as well. 'This was a casual affair,' said one. 'a short fling at most. What happened is nothing like the way it has been painted. This was never a secret like it has been presented. Pete just decided not to go public because it was not serious. Pete is a red-blooded male, not a monk. She's an attractive girl, with a great body. They had sex a couple of times, but that was it. She was never smuggled into his house or anything like what has been written. This experience has put Pete off dating for a while. In fact, it has probably put him back months in terms of finding a new girlfriend.'

In the longer term, in fact, the situation would not impact on Pete's image in the slightest. It was exasperating for Katie, but whatever she did, the public perception remained that because of her incessant desire to compete with her ex, her continued interest in horse riding, the horsey set and what Pete certainly believed was an attraction for her riding teacher, Andrew Gould – something both parties have always steadfastly refuted – and her general tendency to pick rows and score points, sympathy was with him. Unusually for someone so aware of the power of image, Katie had not quite taken on board how negatively the public would react when she ran wild in the aftermath of the split. If Pete hadn't had public support before that episode, he certainly would have done so afterwards. And then there was Alex: he was fast winning the public round, but there was no escaping the fact that he was a contentious figure and not the most obvious choice to replace Pete.

At this point Pete chose to reveal the problems with depression and anxiety that he had had for years. It all started about a decade previously when he was at the height of his career, culminating in a breakdown that hospitalised him. Unsurprisingly, the problems had resurfaced during the breakdown of his marriage.

'You go through all that anxiety and you think it's the end of your life – but it's not,' he said, recalling the occasion when things finally went completely out of control. It was his first full-on panic attack, and others were to follow. 'I woke up at 3am and I felt a hammering in my head. I started panicking and hyperventilating, my hands were sweating and I thought my heart was going to pop out of my body. You think you're having a heart attack. No matter how many times you've had it, every time you think, this is it – I'm going to die.

'There were times when it was so bad that I thought, am I better off [taking his own life]? But you have to look at what's around you. My family were my entire life, and I thought, how are they going to live the rest of their lives? That's what stopped me.'

He had also resorted to medication, not least because he now had his own children and needed to look after them. 'I won't go back [to hospital] because I've got children: they need me and I will always be there for them. I will never go back,' he insisted.

The revelations had the effect of distracting public attention from his ex wife and her new paramour for a time, but it didn't last for long. Still in LA, Katie made the papers simply by taking a stroll the day after

the Oscars party wearing a fur hat, despite the fact
that the LA climate was as balmy as it had ever been.
The public couldn't get enough of her and the
relationship with Pete was beginning to seem like
ancient history: Katie and Alex were well and truly the
couple to watch now.

CHAPTER TWO
THE REAL KATIE PRICE

So just who were they, the couple who so intrigued the nation? For Katie and Alex had become the subject of complete fascination, quite as much as Katie and Pete ever had been. Katie was capable of attracting a huge amount of attention on her own, of course, with no need of help from anyone else, while Alex had, until meeting her, been very much an unknown quantity. But together, they were far more than the sum of their parts: an erstwhile glamour model turned businesswoman and a male model, now an actor and a cage fighter. What were their stories and how had they got to where they were today?

Katrina Amy Alexandria Alexis Infield Price was

born in Newport, Wales, on 22 May 1978, the second child of Amy and Ray Infield. She has an older brother, Daniel. Shortly afterwards, the family moved to Brighton in Sussex, the area in which Katie has lived for most of her life. She was only four years old when her parents split up and nine when her mother remarried, to Paul Price, with whom she went on to have another daughter, Sophie. Katie took Paul's surname, and it is he who acted as a father when she was growing up.

The young Katie had a fairly normal childhood, becoming obsessed with horses, an enthusiasm that lasts till this day. 'I didn't really want to be only a glamour model,' she said in an interview in 2005; post her very successful stint in the *I'm A Celebrity...* jungle, in which she met Pete. 'I'm happy that I am, though. I've made a lot of money – I still make a lot of money. Who'd say no to that? When I used to tell people I wanted to be a pop star, they'd all say "Yeah, yeah, great", but they were messing me around. Now I've got a new management company and my boyfriend Pete, and it's all happening for me.'

Her childhood was not unmarked by trauma, though. When Katie was just six years old, she was subjected to a sexual assault. It does not take a professional psychiatrist to see that this might have coloured her views on men – she never appears to trust any of her partners completely and constantly gives the impression that she wants to get one over them, which may well date back to the time of the attack.

Katie was playing in a park with a friend from school when it happened. A man approached them and offered to buy ice creams: however, he then exposed himself and began touching the two little girls. Both were so terrified that they didn't scream or run away, and it was only the intervention of some older children that put a stop to what was going on. The man fled and has never been found.

This story came into the public domain when Katie went on Piers Morgan's talk show and she herself admits that it may well have had a long-term effect on her relationships with men. 'Compose. Hang on. It's all right – I'm strong. Compose,' she said, as she related the tale. 'Some weirdo! Oh, you know what I'm saying, just some weirdo in a park. Well, it's never affected me, but obviously it must have done for me to just feel like that. But I don't know. You just learn to get on with things, don't you? I haven't got a problem normally with it, so I don't know why I do have a problem with it now. But anyway…'

Life improved considerably in 1988 when Amy married Paul. They sent the young Katie to Blatchington Mill Secondary School, where she excelled at sports, especially riding, which in turn made her determined to succeed as an adult – to have all the things she couldn't have as a child.

'I was only happy when I was with horses,' she admitted. 'My mum couldn't afford for me to go to the Pony Club. I had the ugliest, hairiest pony in the yard and you'd get girls with really nice ponies and their mum and dad involved. They were all posh girls. I just come from a normal family, working class: I didn't own a horse – I had it on loan. He was 18 years old, 14 hands, bay, and he was called Star.'

Today, Katie owns a whole stable full of horses. Again, the childhood marked what the adult became.

In her teens, Katie transformed into a looker. She was not remotely academic and although obsessed with horses, didn't see that leading to a career and so modelling began to seem like the obvious way to make her mark. However, yet again Katie had an unpleasant experience with a man – if the childhood incident hadn't done enough to turn her against the male of the species, then this next would seem to have done the trick – this time in the guise of a photographer who went on to be convicted for child-sex offences. Again, the story came out on the Piers Morgan show. Katie was only 13 when she went to the studio to have some initial shots taken and yet another unpleasant experience ensued.

'Muggins here, who didn't know that, then paid for

this course,' Katie told Piers. 'Well, my mum did. He was the photographer on it and I felt really comfy with him. He said, "Oh, I've got other jobs for you," and he was friendly with my mum and he was so legit with everything. He said, "I will take some pictures of you at my house." He never let my mum stay. It was at his mum and dad's house he done the pictures. My mum didn't know what kind of pictures he was going to take and neither did I. You just wouldn't think. He was with another lady, as well. He used to do pictures of me in a bikini, sticking my tongue out at the camera, and then another time he wanted to put a shirt on me. This is when the woman was there. And they said, "We want to put it on you, but we want you naked." When you are that young you think, oh, I'll do anything just to be a model.'

Unsurprisingly, the shoot went nowhere, and for a short time Katie led a pretty uneventful life, working in a care home. However, she was on the verge of training to become a nurse when fate intervened. The *Sun* came across a couple of pictures of the would-be model and got in touch: it was while talking to them that it was decided that Katie would go under the name of Jordan. This she duly did, the pictures appeared and a new Page 3 girl was born.

Katie was not the first topless model in the family – that honour went to her grandmother – but she quickly showed some indefinable quality that made it obvious she would stand out from the rest. While most Page 3 girls have a pretty short professional lifespan, Katie was quickly to prove herself in a brand new league: she was pretty, obviously, but then, most Page 3 girls are. She was also prepared to work hard, but that wasn't totally unusual, either. In fact, what was beginning to emerge were two qualities: an absolute determination to make it to the top and stay there, come what may, and a certain, indefinable empathy. In the early days, Katie's fans were almost entirely male, but as time went on she began to appeal to both sexes, not least because women felt they could relate to her. Katie had had more than her fair share of upset and heartbreak, including, in more recent years, a child with health problems and a divorce, but her modus operandi has always been to get on with it. Women sympathised with that attitude and respected it, too. And then there was the feeling that she is, in many ways, 'one of us' – an ordinary girl-next-door made good.

Not that Katie wasn't determined to help herself in every way she could along the path to fame. Nature had endowed her with a B measurement in the chest area, but as she embarked on her career in glamour modelling, Katie was to have the first of numerous operations, which took her up first to a D and finally, an FF.

'I always felt that I looked flat-chested when I stood next to other girls on the glamour circuit,' she admitted. 'I was a nervous wreck when Warren [then boyfriend Warren Furman] took me to the hospital and really started panicking when the doctor came in and drew, in felt-tip pen, where he was going to cut. I was convinced the anaesthetic wouldn't work and I'd feel everything. I was so scared that when they tried to put me out, I wouldn't go under. I almost broke the doctor's hand because I was squeezing it so much.'

In fact, Katie was to overcome her fears so successfully that this would be the first of innumerable operations to change her appearance, for she is unrecognisable now, compared to the early days. When Katie first appeared on the scene, she was fresh-faced, blonde and almost wholesomely pretty: it is only recently that her hair has been jet black, her cheeks artificially plumped. But she was determined to change her appearance, and so next up, was a nose job. 'It was fine before, but the doctor was a perfectionist and I said if you could change anything about me, what would it be? And he said my nose, so I just did it,' she revealed, some years earlier. 'You can buy designer outfits – I just bought a designer nose. It's not everybody's cup of tea having surgery, but I'm not planning to have any more.'

Of course, this was not a resolution that she would maintain.

The Katie of today was beginning to emerge, although ironically, her decision to have breast enlargement surgery brought to an end her stint at the *Sun* – the newspaper had a policy of using only completely natural models. But Katie was getting to a stage where she didn't need them any more, anyway. That indefinable quality was already very much in evidence and now she featured in the gossip columns, whether or not she posed for Page 3. She was becoming a stalwart in men's magazines, guest presented *The Big Breakfast* and played herself in *Dream Team*. In 2001, she ran under her real name as the candidate for Stretford and Urmston in the General Election – 'For a Bigger and Betta Future'. After promising free breast implants, more nudist beaches and a ban on parking tickets, she won 1.8 per cent of the vote.

It was around this time that Katie made the transition to more mainstream fame. Of course, it was to be a few years hence before she finally shed the glamour image, courtesy of the jungle, but she was now beginning to appear regularly in the gossip columns, not least because she had a tendency to choose boyfriends who were in the public eye. They included Teddy Sheringham, *Pop Idol* Gareth Gates,

Gladiator Ace (Warren Furman), Dane Bowers and Dwight Yorke.

It had been serious with Ace, but he couldn't take the reality of her glamour career; she was then with Dane for a couple of years. It was with Dane that Katie experienced the first real rough and tumble of a celebrity pairing: she discovered that she was pregnant with his child, but decided on an abortion when she learned that he'd been cheating on her. There followed an overdose: 'It was probably just to get his attention,' she admitted afterwards. 'Stupid. I don't recommend it to anyone – it doesn't get you anywhere.'

It didn't help that Dane had started working with Victoria Beckham. For a start, Katie suspected that he fancied Victoria at some level and secondly, she herself had wanted a musical career and here was her own boyfriend helping someone else. Dane appeared increasingly dissatisfied, too. 'He changed,' said Katie. 'He used to say, "Why can't we be like Victoria and David?" like the way they were in love – which I thought we were. He just kept comparing everything.'

Ultimately, the two were to split, but Katie would fare even worse the next time around. In 2001, she met the Manchester United player (and teammate of David Beckham) Dwight Yorke, who was 27 to Katie's 23. Almost from the start, the signs were there that it was going to go wrong. At almost the exact time that Katie discovered she was pregnant with her oldest child – who was to be called Harvey – she discovered that Dwight was interested in the television presenter Gabrielle Richens. 'She has no idea how serious my relationship with Dwight is,' snapped Katie. 'I am expecting his child in April and we had planned to raise it together. Now I have no idea what to think or what to do. I'm devastated.'

After discovering she was pregnant with Dane Bowers' child, Katie had opted for an abortion. This time around, however, she decided to go it alone. She was beginning to make serious money and it was apparent that she did not actually need a man to help her raise the baby – financially, at least. 'I thought, you know what? I'm successful,' she said. 'I've got money. It's not like I can't bring up a child.' From pretty much that moment on, Dwight was off the scene – although in the course of her pregnancy, Katie did manage to fit in a fling with Gareth Gates.

While it gave joy to Katie in the form of her first child, the birth of Harvey also brought problems in its wake. The baby was only six weeks old when doctors discovered he was blind: he had septo-optic dysplasia, a condition that would cause him a great many problems. But Katie was magnificent. Right from the start, she talked about Harvey as being a gift; that she had somehow been placed on earth to look after him. 'It's not a challenge,' she said. 'It's just part of life. It's like, deal with it – that's just me, that's my life. If someone is disabled, they are obviously put on this earth for a reason. I don't know, obviously I was meant to have a child like that. I think what is meant to be, will be without sounding religious about it, because I am not religious at all. In a way, I'm glad – I wouldn't change Harvey for anything.'

One of the reasons why other women came to empathise with Katie was that, like Princess Diana and the late Jade Goody, patently she had not enjoyed a charmed life. Being dumped by the father of her child before discovering that child was going to have severe difficulties was bad enough, but she then discovered that she had a rare form of cancer – leiomyosarcoma (LMS), which attacks the smooth muscle cells in the body. Troubles, in this case, were very much coming in threes.

The problem, signified by a small lump on the hand, came when Katie was still pregnant with Harvey and having a manicure. 'It was tiny, but she [the beautician] still thought it felt odd and suggested I had it looked at,' recalled Katie. '[My GP] took one look at the lump and immediately expressed concern. Then he referred me to a specialist in Hove. Mr Williams was equally concerned and wanted the lump to be cut out and analysed immediately but I wanted to wait until after Harvey had arrived.'

Could anything more have gone wrong at that time? Katie was a tough woman, but even she must have wondered what fate had in store for her next. 'The doctor sat me down immediately,' she continued. 'I could tell from his face that something wasn't right. Then he came right out with it. He said, "Kate, I've got bad news: it's cancer." I almost laughed, but just sat staring at him as he went into a more detailed explanation of what they'd found. I think I took in about 30 per cent of it. When he stopped, I asked if the cancer could have been the cause of Harvey's blindness. He said absolutely not.'

It might, however, have been exacerbated by the pregnancy. 'Mr Williams also said it was almost certain that another lump would return and that I'd need more treatment,' said Katie. 'I just sat there nodding, not taking it in at all. I was couldn't feel anything, couldn't think anything, couldn't even cry. When I got outside, I told Clare and [my then boyfriend] Matt – they immediately assumed I was making some kind of sick joke. Then I rang my mum.'

Ultimately, of course, the treatment proved successful and by 2003, Katie was well again. In the meantime, public perception of her was beginning to change. 'I don't want sympathy from people 'cos of what happened, you know,' she insisted. 'I'm strong and I'm good at dealing with things, there's far worse-off people than me. My son's blind – whatever – he doesn't know any different. There's no point crying, is there? People worry too much. Life would be boring if we're all the same. Is that the wrong attitude to have? Anyway, women are all on my side now: since they found out about Harvey and me having the old cancer bollocks...' It was hard not to admire her approach.

Boyfriends continued to come and go: the latest being Scott Sullivan. A millionaire's son who, in fact, bore a distinct resemblance to Alex Reid, Scott and Katie became an item in 2003, with Scott moving in to her Sussex abode and taking on a paternal role towards Harvey, as Pete was shortly also to do. The two were happy enough for a while, but Scott was a bit of a playboy and as such, unlikely to last the course, for while Katie might have raised eyebrows more than once in connection with her long-term boyfriends, the men she chose to marry were more home-loving types.

Those closest to her realised the truth of this as well. 'Scott's a nice enough lad, but he's definitely not the one,' said her stepfather Paul. 'He's too much of a playboy – he's always on holiday, messing about. He just lives off his parents' money. He's too young and he's not ready to settle down. Kate's got baby Harvey to think about: she needs some stability in her life, but she's not going to get it from him. Me and Kate's mum have both dropped hints, but Kate's her own woman.'

She was indeed, and at the beginning of 2004 Katie had a new project on the go – one that would change her life in ways that she could not have previously imagined. She had agreed to star in the latest series of *I'm A Celebrity... Get Me Out Of Here!*, the show in which the famous and the not-so-famous spend several weeks in the Australian jungle, being asked to perform unspeakable tasks in return for food. Tough as old boots, Katie was the perfect contender, and so she went in.

Katie approached the show as she always approached everything: brash enthusiasm mixed with a certain earthy humour. 'I quite enjoyed having a snake slithering over my boobs and I've had worse things on me – I've slept with Dane Bowers,' she declared. 'I work around horses a lot, so I'm used to rats, too. And nothing in that jungle could be a bigger rat than my son Harvey's father, Dwight Yorke. The only thing Scott's said I can't do is sleep with Peter Andre. He said I can sling my hook if I do, as I will have brought shame on myself for bedding a man who has that bad a haircut.'

Little could Scott – or anyone else – have known.

Of course, it was to be the start of the great romance with Pete, but no one else clocked that at the time. Pete himself had all but fallen off the British national radar: after a short career as a pop star in the mid 1990s, he had retreated from the scene and was by then living in Cyprus, where his family originally came from. His inclusion on the show roused a modicum of interest, but no one really thought it would lead to anything. Indeed, far more interest was paid to Kerry Katona – at that point still married to Westlife's Brian McFadden, who would to go on to be crowned Queen of the Jungle as the show's eventual winner – and John Lydon, aka Johnny Rotten of the Sex Pistols. He and Katie indulged in frequent spats – 'Take your implants out of my face!' – he fumed at one point, before storming off from the show early. But although this provoked some interest in viewers, the real intrigue lay elsewhere.

And the real interest, of course, was Katie and Pete. They seemed to hit it off right from the start, although initially both were dubious about the other's intentions: were they flirting (and they were certainly doing so increasingly) because they were really attracted to one another? Or was each using the other to attract the camera's attention and so further their respective careers?

Initially, perhaps, it was a bit of both but it wasn't long before the attraction was obviously very real. Kerry Katona had assumed the role of unofficial go-between, drawing both of them out into admitting they fancied one another: 'You can see you're physically attracted to her,' she told Pete. 'You definitely want a piece of cake, you do. Come on, be a man and admit it! Who wouldn't? Kate's a woman. All women play. You're only human. F*****g hell, I'm female and I want a part of her!'

As this was happening, something else was becoming apparent as well. Until then, Katie had been seen as not a great deal more than a glamour model who went out with footballers and pop stars and spent much of her time falling out of nightclubs, and although there had been a great deal of sympathy about Harvey, that was still how she was perceived to be. Now, however, she was coming across as something else. She was increasingly obviously a good sport, undertaking any trial that she had to undergo with gusto, a person who did not sit around complaining about her lot. That, and her on-screen dalliance with Pete was drawing in the viewers in droves: she was transforming from Jordan into Katie Price in front of the viewer's very eyes.

And the fact that she was nominally still with Scott didn't seem to be holding anyone back. Indeed, Katie appeared increasingly unhappy with her man. 'I'm not happy with my boyfriend,' she told the other celebrities present. 'He's not my boyfriend, as far as I'm concerned at the minute. He hasn't wished me luck, hasn't texted me for two/three days. Nothing...' Scott, on the other hand, was growing increasingly panicky about what was happening up there on the nation's television screens: just as Alex was to do when Katie returned to the jungle more than five years later, he rather impetuously rushed to Australia, but all to no avail.

Once out of the jungle, a three-way game of cat and mouse appeared to take place. On the one hand, Katie and Pete did not appear to be entirely sure that the other was taking the nascent relationship seriously, and so they dodged around each other, wanting to meet and yet neither seemed prepared to show their hand. On the other, the two appeared to be playing with the media: all sorts of lurid tales about whether they had or hadn't slept together were being leaked, as was speculation about whether they were now a serious couple or indeed, actually having a relationship at all. In time, of course, it became patently obvious that not only were they indeed an item, but one that was going to last the distance – at least for a while.

'I'm devastated by what Katie's been up to with

Peter,' revealed Scott, while the two were still in situ in the jungle. 'It's eating away at me all the time – the thought of whether it's all an act for the cameras or if there's something really going on. What's worse is that I'm sure Katie must realise what she's doing is going to upset me, but she doesn't seem to care. I'm still clinging to the hope that this is all a stunt and part of her game plan to win. I don't know what's going to happen between us – I hope we can work it out, but no matter how far she goes, I'll forgive her. Katie's just too special to me to let go of without a fight.'

But matters had gone much too far for that: Katie and Pete were now an item, although even from the beginning there seemed to be some awareness that there were two sides to the lady herself – Katie *and* Jordan – and Pete had only fallen for one of them. But at the time, it didn't seem to matter for they were young and in love. Very quickly, it was apparent that even if Pete had been a player in the past, he was now taking his new relationship seriously enough to become a father figure for Harvey, while Katie, too, at last seemed ready to settle down. Jordan was just an act: the real woman was about to come to the fore.

'Jordan is a slag, slut and bitch,' revealed Katie. 'Kate likes to stay at home, curl up in front of the fire and play with her son. The problem I've had is the Jordan side has started to take over my life. It's an act, but it's out of control. I realised that if I'm going to make a relationship last it's going to be as Kate, not Jordan. He has told me he's fallen for Kate, the real me. Not Jordan, the glamour girl I invented. She is gone, dead. I want more children, a proper family with the man I love – that's Peter.'

And so it was to prove, the only fly in the ointment being Scott. He was utterly (and understandably) livid, coming across somewhat as the spectre at the feast. While Katie and Pete became increasingly absorbed in each other, he ranted and raved at what had taken place. 'She's hurt me so much,' he said. 'I've been humiliated in front of the world. I'm totally confused. Peter is a total slimeball and I'm embarrassed she's gone off with such a first-class tosser.'

But no one else saw Pete in that light: rather, he quickly came across as exactly what he was, namely charming and amiable. And so he and Katie started on the first of their many reality shows, and marriage and the two children soon followed. At first, all was peace and domestic harmony: Katie, keen to pursue a singing career, attempted to be selected to represent Britain in the 2005 Eurovision Song Contest, but it didn't quite work out. A year later, she and Pete then released an album of duets but it too did not really take off.

By this time, however, Katie was becoming a brand as much as a person. Clothes ranges for children and adults, Pony Club books, underwear appeared and through her various endorsements and sponsorships, she was becoming seriously rich. Behind the scenes all was not well, however. Katie's great passion in life was horses and she now had a stable full of her own, but this was beginning to cause rows. Pete never felt completely at home with the horsey, country set and was increasingly upset by his wife's closeness to her riding instructor, Andrew Gould. Andrew was married, and while there has never been the slightest suggestion that anything improper occurred between him and Katie, tensions were building up, becoming all too much.

And so, finally, matters came to a head and the fairytale was over. Determined to block out the pain, Katie threw herself into hedonistic pursuits. A wild week in Ibiza followed, along with a couple of short-term flings, increasingly public and bitter rows with Pete, a split from her management company and, it seemed, a brief fall from grace.

But Katie was not destined to be on her own for long. In July 2009, she met the man who was to become her second husband, with whom she could enjoy a fresh start and a new future. After some months of appearing gaunt and strained, she started to loosen up and returned to her old self, happy once more. But just who really was Alex Reid?

CHAPTER THREE
ALONG CAME ALEX

It is a fact of Katie's more recent years that the men she has taken up with have seen their lives completely turned around by association, and nowhere is this more true than of the men she has married. Around the time he met Katie, Pete went from being a washed-up pop star who now owned a gym in Cyprus to one of the most popular and best-loved entertainers in Britain and to the astonishment of many, exactly the same thing appears to be happening with Alex Reid.

When he first came on the scene, Katie's fans were rather dismayed by tales of cross dressing and cage fighting, but as time goes on, public feeling has been warming to him to the extent that he has even been touted as possibly the next James Bond. Just like Pete, a reality television show – in this case, *Celebrity Big Brother* – transformed his image. And just as with Pete, he and Katie together as a couple are far more than the sum of their relevant parts.

Alex Aristides Reid was born in Aldershot, Hampshire, on 21 August 1975 to Carol and Bob, a paratrooper. The youngest of six siblings, three boys and three girls, he says that the presence of his brother Rupert stopped him from being babied. 'He's older by four years and he was the baby,' Alex explained. 'I come along, he didn't like it so everyone spoilt him to make up for it.'

Sibling rivalry aside, Alex had a happy, uncomplicated childhood that set him up well for the years ahead. 'I'd go out and play in mud and dirt and [be] adventurous,' he said. 'Kids don't do that these days. Because we know… I don't believe anything's changed over the years, but now we know about paedophiles and nasty people. Parents don't want to let their kids go out. I used to go out and do all sorts of crazy things. Kids don't do it now.'

Right from the start, Alex was a sporty little boy. 'As a young tearaway, I often found myself in many scrapes,' he later recalled. 'I wasn't so much a bully, but having grown up with *Star Wars*, He-Man and Action Force(Man), in my imagination I was a kind of super hero, and so big, small, tough, weak, all found themselves challenged by my incredible ego. Pre-puberty, I was pretty much the toughest kid around (so I thought!). My rude awakening came at about 13 to 14 at senior school, where all of a sudden the kids got tougher and my usual high status was threatened. I had lost the title and didn't like it one bit. Having got a bit chubby and seeing my brother start bodybuilding, I was inspired to work out. Sylvester Stallone was my hero at the time. The next logical step was to start a deadly martial art, so I could again regain my status.' So began the enthusiasm for martial arts, an interest that was to provide him with an exciting career.

In fact, right from the outset Alex was interested in two different arenas: martial arts and acting. In 1996, at the age of 21, he joined the Territorial Army – specifically, 10 Para – which in turn helped him to build up his nascent acting career. 'We referred to ourselves as "The Tenth Jedi Knights",' he later recalled. 'My life now took on a new meaning – I was part of Britain's elite infantry regiment. Enough said. As for acting, it helped no end. Just think how many films [and] TV shows there are about, or using soldiers. Whether it was being a Roman Centurion, a medieval Knight or a World War II US Ranger, film producers want authenticity, so ex reserves or regular forces are regularly used in such productions.'

It was, however, a measure of Alex's determination that he was able to stay in the Paras for some years, while others dropped out – in fact, he left after three years, but not because of the toughness of the training schedule – and that he was able to see that his chosen paths would positively impact on each other. Alex had actually picked two extremely competitive areas – acting and fighting – in which to make his mark, but he was determined to make an impact. He just wasn't entirely sure what form this would take.

But he was certainly determined. The training was very tough. Asked of his memories of that time, Alex said later: 'Training so hard I blacked out, getting knocked down by black sashes, week after week; going through walking, kick and punch drills for hours on end and wanting to cry, but not being allowed to as not to show weakness. Looking back, other than having to learn complicated forms the training was pretty basic, but bloody hard!'

Being fighting fit was not enough, however. In 1996, Alex entered and won Storm Model Management's annual competition: a brief modelling career ensued, which he didn't enjoy – 'I felt like a piece of meat.' In actual fact, he had done a bit of modelling before, but now he wanted to join a much bigger outfit and see where that would go. To supplement his income, he was doing a small number of dead-end jobs and was eager to branch out far more.

'I was already a model with a smaller agency, but things weren't really happening,' he recalled. 'Then I won that contract and decided to get serious, giving up my crummy jobs as a furniture deliverer and general labourer. It was scary but exciting. I had to learn about signing on and being really skint. I had casting after casting, commuting all over London. What little money I had earned soon went. As for jobs, a few catwalk fashion shows, girly magazines... in the two years I gave it my all I didn't really amount to much, but I did gain experience and the knowledge that I didn't want to be a model any more.'

At least he knew what he didn't want to do, but what he did want to do was act. After landing the part of Tom Hanks' body double in *Saving Private Ryan*, Alex realised that he needed further training if he was to pursue an acting career and so in 1998, he enrolled at the Guildford School of Acting. He only did one year, although he would have liked to do more – funds didn't allow – but even so, this bore fruit. It led to a very small role in *Soldier, Soldier*, and with it, his first real exposure to the industry he was to make his own.

'The assistant directors and production coordinators

began to know me,' he later recalled of his time on the show. It was to prove an enjoyable experience. 'I made myself work by hanging around the director when I saw him wanting an extra to do something in particular. I'd be hovering around just at the right moment. "Hey Alex, do you wanna drive through here?"… "Sven, jump over that wall into that stream!" (I got the nickname Sven for being the biggest pervert.) While I was on *Soldier, Soldier* I couldn't do wrong: if I fell over in shit, I'd get up smelling of roses – I think because I was friends with everyone, including the other extras because most were real soldiers, the actors because that's what I wanted to do, and the crew because I was cheeky but always reliable.' Many years later, those qualities would stand him in good stead as Alex emerged into the limelight, courtesy of Katie, and began to turn into a bona fide star.

Indeed, Alex was learning a good deal about film-making, even if he wasn't able to put it to particularly good use for a time. He might have taken humble roles through his various forays into film making, but he was also working with some of the world's most famous directors and learning his trade as he went along.

'Having worked on many films up to that point, I had seen many different production styles, some very good, but painstakingly slow (Stanley Kubrick, three weeks for a couple of shots!), to the not so good, almost amateurish, does anyone know what's going on here?' he said, recalling the time when he worked on *Saving Private Ryan* with its director, Steven Spielberg. 'But DreamWorks, Spielberg's team, were the best and still are, in my experience. Professional and economic, things get done. Steven doesn't have to get riled if something isn't working – which it sometimes doesn't – everyone around him does the huffing and puffing. People just worked harder, like it was their reputation or honour. It may sound like a horrible atmosphere but on the contrary, it was really cool.'

As time went on, Alex began to rethink other areas of his life. He had remained a member of the Territorial Army, but now left, seemingly because he just didn't have the necessary mindset to make it work. 'My ideals changed,' he explained. 'When I first joined I was all gung-ho, green and keen. I wanted to do everything, even go regular SAS. I was fighting for democracy, for good. My problem is I'm too sensitive – I never showed it, but things do affect me. Not that I couldn't handle the Para mentality: I lived and breathed it, I was a true Para nut. But I think too much, and so in a way began to not fit in.

'I'm not saying Paras are stupid – far from it, you have to be highly intelligent to serve with them – but it's a way of thinking, a social conditioning. And I believe you need it to do the job. Someone has to do the nasty stuff. But killing for freedom for all that is right is one thing, but I became disillusioned with us here in the West's actual moral stand.'

In some ways, it helped that the set-up of his TA unit changed. 'After three years of being involved in everything, my attendance started to dwindle,' he continued. 'Then in 1999, 10 Para was disbanded and made 10-company, part of 4Para so those who were seen as non-regular attendees or not essential for the new role went. This was also a scary period because Serbia was kicking off again. Thank God it all calmed down, but this being pre-disbandment, 10 Para was on standby. It could have been an interesting year. To sum up, other things in my life became more important. My mission on earth became clearer: change this world we live in to a better place through educating rather than killing, or telling stories through acting.'

He also appeared on *Gladiators* – the second of Katie's men to do so. Shortly afterwards, Alex got his first real shot at stardom before meeting Katie: the role of Jason Cunliffe in the Channel 4 soap *Hollyoaks*, which he played between 2001 and 2002. For him, it was an ideal role: Jason was a footballer and the other half of *Hollyoaks*' 'Posh and Becks' with his girlfriend, Geri Hudson. However, Jason is also a player, embroiled in an on-off fling with his publisher Alyson (Sarah Jayne Steed) while also prepared to make a pass at Geri's friend Izzy Cornwell (Elize du Toit). Ultimately, it turns into something of a morality tale: Geri manages to get Jason to marry her and then later kicks him out of her car, determined to punish him by gaining every penny in their divorce settlement, thus ending Alex's time on the series.

There followed sporadic bit parts, but for a time it seemed as if *Hollyoaks* was to be the pinnacle of his career. Alex was once asked about the work he'd done. '*Jonathan Creek*, I was "Diet Coke man" for an episode,' he recalled. '*Tomorrow Never Dies*, I was a Dutch policeman who lets Pierce/Bond out of a car and into a casino party; *Merlin*, Arthurian TV adaptation with Rutger Hauer; *The Saint* with Val Kilmer – played a Russian soldier – and in *The Magic of Movies*, an American GI as well. *Eyes Wide Shut*, this was real fun to film – for anyone who's seen the film, I'll let you use your imagination!'

But ultimately it wasn't very satisfactory stuff: Alex had gone into the business to make a name for himself – which he clearly wasn't doing – and he began to get fed up. 'I could really go on forever, as for two years I worked pretty solidly,' he continued. 'I started off like most extras, trying to get seen in front of the camera, and I would proudly tell everyone to watch this or that. After a short period, the novelty ran off. If you blinked, half the time you'd miss me. That wasn't fame, I wanted more, and I want even more now! I was beginning to get fed up, I was going to be the star!'

At this stage, he was still keen to become an actor, but once he left *Hollyoaks*, almost nothing else turned up. And so, always fit and healthy, ex-TA and in training for years, he increasingly turned to fighting, with varying degrees of success. 'Nothing. Nothing at all,' he said of his acting career at that stage. 'And that was humbling. Fighting was paying more bills than acting. So, I didn't turn my back on acting, I just put it to one side. I thought, concentrate on the fighting – which is a bit like acting, anyway. It's a performance, it's a competition and you're entertaining. Like Russell Crowe said in *Gladiator*: "Are you entertained?" – you know. And competing in an arena, it is a show, and it can be like going on stage. It's just that it's painful if it goes wrong.'

Strangely enough, given his profession Alex did not consider himself to be a particularly aggressive person, which is perhaps why he later came across so well on *Celebrity Big Brother*. Instead, he coped with what he was doing in the ring by entering 'The

Zone'. Though he did not exactly want to hurt his opponent as such, he was keen to beat him, and if hurting him was an unfortunate byproduct – well, it had to be done.

'For me, it's about being in the moment,' he revealed. 'Maybe it's not a fight, maybe I'm playing tennis – or making sushi. I'm so into it, making the perfect sushi. Doing the perfect whatever it is – business deal, whatever. That's the secret: I'm performing the perfect technique.'

Even then, he still had to take on any number of other jobs to get by. For some time, he worked on the doors of nightclubs, where his physique and training stood him in good stead. This was not a period that he looked back on with any degree of fondness, though. Asked his opinion of street brawling in 2002, he gave a surprisingly down-to-earth answer: 'My honest opinion – being very, very rich, dressed in a smart Armani suit,' he told one interviewer. 'When trouble comes your way, you won't even know about it – your bodyguards sort it! At worst you may have to click your fingers! I don't miss door work one bit. It served its purpose: I was lucky (sensible) to have avoided many fights, although I could bore you with how tough I am in the scraps I have had, which I won't. Street brawling, I just don't understand it – I've done it myself, it's just stupid and no one really wins.

Repercussions? Hearsay? Pride? Police?' It was a very down-to-earth attitude, which he shared with his future bride.

And that, for many years to come, was that. Always hopeful of getting back into acting, Alex toured the world as a fighter, built up a reputation and won roughly half the fights he engaged in. At the same time he had a serious, long-term relationship – as well as a couple of flings. His girlfriend for ten years, until Katie came along, was a childhood sweetheart – a teacher called Marie Thornett. In truth, everyone had expected the pair to wed.

But there were in fact a number of other women in his life throughout the years and the relationship with Marie was not always at the forefront of his mind. Ultimately his relationship with Marie survived – until Katie came along. Then, in an odd rerun of the scenario when Scott Sullivan found himself turfed out as soon as Peter Andre showed up, Marie suddenly found herself surplus to requirements and she was quite as angry as Scott had been.

'What those two have done to me is cruel beyond words,' she declared. 'They've thought of nobody but themselves. I've cried almost non-stop since I found out. I can never forgive them. Alex was supposed to be with me in Spain, instead he was groping her in a nightclub. We planned to spend the rest of our lives together and now it's in ruins, thanks to Jordan. Going out with Jordan is going to help Alex realise both those fantasies [of fame].'

Indeed, she was adamant they were all set to wed. 'There's no doubt about it, we both felt that way,' she continued. 'We were a family unit, and Alex was great with my son. We'd often talk about the future, getting married and having children. I wanted nothing more. Often Alex would spot a lovely house and ring me to say, "I've driven past our future home." I want to be nasty about them but I can't, I'm just too upset. Even after everything he has done to me, I hope he is happy and achieves the fame he craves. I hope he makes Jordan happy and fulfils what she's missing, but I don't think he will ever love her like he loved me. I'll never take him back now. Alex broke my heart and Jordan is welcome to him.'

Alex and Marie (who came from Aldershot) first met in 1999 and quickly became an item. But Alex wasn't the only one who cultivated other interests: in 2006, there was a separation, which at that time turned out not to be permanent, but resulted in Marie becoming pregnant. She subsequently gave birth to a boy, but the two were reunited until the advent of Katie – and an increasingly incandescent Marie.

'Alex has only one real love and that's himself,' Marie declared in the aftermath of the break-up.

'Fame and fortune are what drives him. We used to snuggle up and watch Katie and Peter Andre's TV show. He used to joke he'd get with her for the money and then come back to me. It's definitely not funny now. He's vain and vacuous, I believe they are made for each other.'

Marie had been very hurt, obviously, and it cannot have been easy to accept the fact that far from Alex being in it for the money, the relationship with Katie was very real. But there had been a crossover period, when he appeared to have been caught between the two women, and perhaps he didn't handle it as well as he might have.

In fact, Marie had been on holiday in Majorca – Alex wasn't with her because he had to stay at home to prepare for a fight. 'We stayed in regular text contact through the week,' she recalled. 'On July 18 he texted saying how he wished he could be with me. It was only a few days later, when I got home, I discovered that was the day of Michelle Heaton's birthday party where he first got it on with Jordan. That was so cruel of him.'

Initially Alex, probably panic-stricken, failed to return her calls. He did, however, send her a text saying, 'I care about you and always will.' But he was still very publicly with Katie, causing – if truth be told – rather harsh feelings. 'I was shocked to the core when

I found out,' said Marie. 'It was so sneaky.' But the relationship was now finally at an end.

As so often happens, though, when a person first becomes well known, more details about Alex's love life began to emerge and it turned out that Katie was far from the first other woman in his life. Early in 2009, he also had a fling with Jodie Mugridge, a PR girl he met while working as a doorman at the Remix Club in Woking, Surrey. She sounded every bit as irate as Marie (who she was unaware that Alex was still involved with). And there were certain elements of her story, not least the obsession with his own appearance, which made her account of her time with Alex somewhat familiar.

'It was a bit frustrating to catch him constantly trying to sneak a glimpse of himself in the mirror on my wardrobe door,' she snapped. 'And he insisted on shaving his entire body and even admitted to having tanning injections.' Nor did the first date go too well. 'As the night went on he got very gropey and made me feel uncomfortable,' she continued. I'm a private sort of person and found his behaviour embarrassing. At the end of the night he drove me home and asked again to spend the night with me. I just said I wasn't that sort of girl.'

Alex's wooing techniques were certainly a little unconventional: he sent a series of text messages, the content of which took Jodie aback. 'He described a graphic sexual fantasy to me that I found totally shocking and revealed he was extremely adventurous,' she recalled. 'I didn't even know how to reply. I think he realised he freaked me out because he toned it down very quickly.'

But that wasn't the end of it. She did see him again – indeed, they had a brief relationship – but Alex once more shocked her by stripping in her mother's sitting room, just as he was to do on *Celebrity Big Brother* early the following year. 'I couldn't believe what I was seeing,' said Jodie with masterly understatement. 'I was expecting to take his coat and offer him a cup of tea, but he was clearly expecting something very different. Everything was on display. Alex never wears pants because he claims that they're uncomfortable and he wasted no time in proving the point. He is a total exhibitionist who is only interested in sex, sex, sex; he was also extremely vocal in bed. No other boyfriend of mine had yelled as loudly as Alex. I hope Jordan has soundproofing! And when he sleeps, he snores like a pneumatic drill.'

Clearly disappointed at the way matters had turned out, she continued: 'Although our relationship was casual I thought we were definitely going to meet up when I was back from holiday but in the meantime he met Jordan. Luckily for me I hadn't fallen in love with him. He would usually turn up in his favourite pair of white slip-on loafers, white linen trousers that were too short or jeans with big chains hanging from his pockets. And he would sometimes leave his mobile phone earpiece in for good measure.

'I thought straight away Alex and Jordan would gel sexually. Jordan will probably enjoy the fact he is all over her at the moment because she needs the attention but there is no way he should have met those children so soon because he won't be able to stop himself from groping her in front of them.'

It was a sentiment Peter Andre appeared to share. He was not at all happy when the relationship became public knowledge and was absolutely livid when it emerged that Junior had seen Alex in Katie's bed but there wasn't a lot he could do.

Nor was that the last of it. Alex was a good-looking man in his thirties and so it was perhaps not surprising that yet another woman came forward now, too. The relationship with Marie had been very on-off and when it was in one of its extended off periods, Alex got together with a kickboxer called Danielle Sims and even moved in with her for a while. They had rather a wild sex life together, which Danielle was only too happy to share with the world once her ex-lover found fame.

'Alex got off on rough sex,' she said. 'He liked to

put his hands around my throat in a stranglehold and say, "Who's the master? Who's the daddy?" He would then tell me I was never going to sleep with anyone else but him – all the time he had his hands round my throat in a grip. Sometimes I'd have to cough or shake my head furiously before he'd release me but it never got to the point where I'd actually pass out.'

And that wasn't the half of it. 'I think he may have met his match in Jordan,' Danielle continued. 'I don't think she'd have any problems in the dominating department. Like Alex, Jordan seems to like dressing up in provocative outfits. One of his favourite fighting outfits included a black leather gimp mask, a pair of leather cowboy chaps and a leather cat-o-nine-tails. Alex used it on his opponent, but after the fight, he used it on my bare bum. Other times, he liked to tie a ball-gag round my mouth to muffle my screams. He'd always position the mirror so he could watch himself during these romps. I hope Jordan knows what she's letting herself in for.

'Alex is very kinky and I think Jordan might have some fun with that. For my birthday, he bought me silk bondage ties, tied me to the bed then did whatever he wanted. One time he took me to the adult exhibition, Erotica. He stocked up on sex toys, including a contraption he could strap to his forehead. He also bought bondage tape to strap me up. Alex told me that at the end of the exhibition they hold a huge sex party run by the world's leading fetish club, Torture Garden. We never went, but Alex told me that he had been before with a friend and it wasn't the place for a girl to go on her own.'

With that background it was hardly surprising that Katie's fans were a little concerned as to what her relationship with her new man might entail, nor were matters helped by the fact that Alex had just starred in a film called *Killer Babe* (originally *Killer Bitch*), which was not only violent and sexually charged, but according to pre-release reviews, supposed to be absolutely dreadful, as well. Then there was the cross-dressing and the fact that Alex was clearly a little kinky, if nothing else. But the fact remained that for all the angry ex-lovers, for all the lurid gossip about what he got up to behind closed doors, and for all the general nonsense being posted about him, when he finally got to talk directly to the public, Alex just didn't seem that bad a bloke. He was plainly besotted with Katie, willing to make an effort with the children and – especially when he went on *Celebrity Big Brother* – gave every impression that he was an amiable cove who could hardly believe his luck, in the nicest possible way.

He wasn't talking in terms of a fling, either. 'I see a serious long-term future together,' he proclaimed. 'I'd love to have kids, it's a big thing with me. You just know sometimes. Sure, I have been a ladykiller. Ten years ago, I had my pick – I probably still could, but this time I've met my match. And I'm grateful to all the other women I've been with because they put me in the position I'm in now. They helped me realise Katie is my ideal woman. We are so alike it's unbelievable. And being in love is amazing. Forget about the money and the fame, just really connecting with someone, that's something else.

'We're both very bright, that's another thing we have in common. I'm really into self-improvement, ancient theology. I think a lot and read. Right now, I'm reading *The Neo-Tech Discovery* – how to live longer and make more money. Katie is super-sharp too.'

Nor did the reports about cross-dressing worry her, either. 'Katie loves it,' asserted Alex. 'I'm just a crazy kind of guy. I don't consider myself a drag queen – I just like dressing up as a woman. I also like to dress up as all sorts – Superman, Sinbad the Sailor, a Ninja warrior, a Jedi knight... I've even got a light sabre in the bedroom! I'm not a pervert or a freak, I just push boundaries in everything I do – I just like to try everything, I'm open to everything. As long as you're not hurting anyone it doesn't matter. I'm very open-minded.'

'A lot of my friends in the fight game are always

getting asked, "Does that Alex Reid wear make-up? Does he try and touch you up when you're training?" They just laugh it off. Tell them I'm an okay bloke and I'm going to be the one laughing at the end of the day. I'm just having fun: it doesn't bother me that Katie is the breadwinner – I'm quite liberated in that respect. The mansion and limos are fun but I provide in this relationship what's needed. And the fact she's so successful inspires me. It's not the reason I'm with her, but I'm not one to knock a gift horse in the mouth – my association with her has definitely helped, I'm more marketable now.'

That was for sure, but Alex came out with it in a remarkably cheery and unselfconscious way. Clearly he wasn't with Katie for the kudos – he was in love.

CHAPTER FOUR

AND PETE MAKES THREE

Of all the trio caught up in the drama that has enthralled the nation, the most reluctant participant has been Peter James Andrea, aka Peter Andre, much-loved pop star and Katie's first husband. Although he has spoken publicly about the breakdown of their relationship and the subsequent worries about what to do about the children, especially now there is a stepfather on the scene, Pete has never given the impression of enjoying the huge amounts of publicity. Indeed, early on in the break-up, he refused to speak directly to Katie at all, on the grounds that anything he said would end up plastered all over the media. Nor did he appear to want to find another partner as quickly as his ex-wife did. Apart from the small embarrassment of the kiss-and-tell, Pete has been remarkably slow to find another girlfriend, let alone a new spouse.

But then, Pete was a few years older than Katie and Alex, and had also experienced more of life's rollercoaster than they had, which made his reticence a little easier to understand. Pete was born on 27 February 1973, the second youngest of six: his parents, Savvas and Thea, of Cypriot extraction, were living in Harrow, London when he was born and his siblings, to whom he remains very close, are Andrew, Chris, Danny, Michael and Debbie.

Savvas has done well for himself. 'He owned 17 properties in England, including Notting Hill and Paddington, before I was born,' Pete revealed. 'My parents came to the UK with nothing. My dad was a barber by trade, which he learned when he was 12. He had to go to a country where he didn't know any English, but he made his way. He became very good and started investing in property, so he always told me to do the same.'

Pete attended Sudbury Junior School but ultimately, however, was brought up in Australia, where his parents moved when he was 6 years old and this was where he first started to make his name. 'We thought we were going on holiday, but we actually left for good,' he later recalled. The family moved to

Southport on Queensland's Gold Coast, actually only about 50 miles away from the celebrity jungle in which he was to meet his future wife. He attended the local school, Keebra Park. His childhood, however, was to prepare him for the vagaries of life that lay ahead.

But this was not a very happy time, not least because he was bullied: 'I used to get picked on for the way I looked because a lot of the kids were blond-haired and blue-eyed,' he recalled. 'It was so hurtful being called names and I felt terribly desperate and lonely at times. I couldn't rat on anybody because it was the ultimate no-no – I'd have been considered weak if I told. I didn't go to my parents because I was ashamed and they would have said something to my teacher. The school would then have acted and I would have been picked on even more for being a "dobber".'

Classmates remember a similar story. 'I'd say he would have hated his school life, because he was a skinny little shit,' said one. 'We used to play basketball, before and after school as well as lunchtime, and he would try to join in, but he was hopeless. He was the wimp who always got picked on.'

He was also the one who would go on to have the last laugh.

It was this less than physically perfect aspect to his

life that first sent Pete to the gym. As he grew older and began to fill out, he also began to grow into his looks, which he was making a big effort to maintain. Matters improved when he went to Benowa High School, while his interest in music was developing: when he was 13, he and his brother Chris wrote the song, 'Dream A Little', which was to go on to appear on his first album. Here, Pete developed his first big crush: Liza Tyler, a fellow classmate. Pete's crush inspired Chris to write a song: 'My brother wrote a song about her because we thought Liza was a good title for a song,' recalled Pete. 'He still plays the song today and Liza has known nothing about it till this very minute!'

Many of the family settled permanently in the area – Debbie has a beauty salon in Varsity Lakes – but Pete was getting restless. He had also set his heart on becoming a star and so in 1990, when he was just 17, he appeared on the Australian version of *New Faces*. He did a cover version of Bobby Brown's 'Don't Be Cruel' – perhaps not his greatest moment ever as a performer, but it was enough to catch the eye of Molly Meldrum, the boss of Melodian Records and one of the judges, who offered him a contract live on air. And so a show business career, Part One, was born.

Before his fame began to spread worldwide, Pete's initial success came in Australia. In 1992, he released the debut single, 'Gimme Little Sign', which was a smash success: it stayed in the ARIA charts (Australia's official music chart) for a staggering 31 weeks, got to number three and also became the biggest-selling single of the year. The following year, Pete released his first album, entitled *Simply, Peter Andre*. More singles followed: 'Funky Junky' and 'Let's Get It On/Do You Wanna Dance' both made the Australian Top 20, while Pete then began to crack the UK market with 'Only One'. By the time he was 23, he was a special guest performer with both Madonna and Bobby Brown: a brilliant future seemed assured.

It was not until 1995, however, that Pete released the song with which he is most associated, 'Mysterious Girl', and even then it took some months of bubbling away before it finally did well in the UK. 'Mysterious Girl' was a reggae song, written by Pete himself, alongside Glen Goldsmith and Philip Jackson, and featuring Bubbler Ranx as a guest vocalist and Champagne Ex on the video, which was filmed in Thailand, and which gave Pete the chance to show off his well toned torso. It did well in the Pacific, reaching number one in New Zealand and number eight in Australia, but initially didn't do so well in the UK. Initially it only got to number 53, until the following year when it finally got to the UK number two slot.

Peter Andre's name was now famous in the land of his birth, as well as the land where he grew up.

Pete was actually making some serious money now, and although it was erroneously believed that by the time he and Katie got together, he didn't have much left, that was not actually the case. Savvas had done well in the UK property market and he was keen that his son should do the same. 'When I first had success in music in the 1990s, he begged me to invest my money,' revealed Pete. 'He said, "When you are young you think that when money is there, it's always going to be there – and it's not. So I invested in properties in Australia and I bought a bit of land in Cyprus, but I didn't buy anything in England. Dad was upset, saying I was spending too much on cars. I'd say that I've invested in Australia, but he told me I should invest in the UK as well.

'My father was my saviour because the money, such as royalties, would come in from Australia and he would just invest it for me. If it had gone into my account, I'd have just spent it – he was always telling me I was spending my money before I had it. When I went into the jungle in 2004, some people may have thought I went in with nothing but unbeknown to the public, I had those investments and I was starting to really do well from them. Merchandising revenue from tours back then was massive. I remember one night at the Royal Albert Hall just in T-shirts I made £20,000! I went into the jungle, thinking, "What have I got to lose?"'

But that was still to come. Back then, what Pete actually had to lose was his career – which he did – and it hit him extremely hard. Initially, it wasn't obvious that matters were about to go belly up: now that he'd finally broken the UK, a couple more hit singles came and went. 'Flava' and 'I Feel You' were both number ones, as well as a number one album, *Natural*, but after this it all began to go wrong. Pete rose to prominence as a pop star, but the move towards R&B was a mistake. The fans didn't much like it, nor did they care very much for his next album, *Time*, which only got to number 28. In 1998 came another single, a cover of 'Kiss the Girl', originally featured in the Disney film *The Little Mermaid*, and that was that for the time being. Pete's record company dropped him and he went back to Cyprus with his tail between his legs.

In later years, Pete very much played this period of his life down, but at the time he was devastated. In fact, for a while he barely knew how to cope. He had gone from being extremely famous and working very hard to right back where he'd started: unknown, but now also forgotten, with a career that seemed well and truly in the past. Pete also spoke later on about the fact that he'd wished he hadn't taken his career so seriously because he found it hard to cope when it all fell away, but at the time it was touch-and-go and he had the breakdown alluded to in the first chapter of this book.

'I was working long hours – I could never say no – so before I knew it, I was working 20-hour days and it all got too much,' he remembered. 'I had 20 [panic attacks] a day and they lasted 25 minutes each. That's a lot of time each day that you're thinking you're going to die. The worst ones are where your body goes into shock – I've had about five of those in my life. That's when your hands lock, your jaw drops, your mouth slopes to one side, you get pins and needles that fill your whole body and you become paralysed for about 15 minutes.'

But it got an awful lot worse once he thought his career was truly at an end. Pete was feeling burned out, so rather than fight back and keep things ticking over, he bowed out of the scene completely and returned to Australia to help out in the family business.

'Well, I got signed up when I was 16, so by the time I was 26 I'd released four albums – only two in the UK – over a 10-year period,' he told one interviewer. 'So I'd been going every day, I was knackered and I just got to a point where I didn't know if I wanted it anymore so I stepped away from it, went to Australia,

Above: She's a celebrity and she got herself out of there – Katie gives an interview after leaving the jungle reality show.

© *ITV/Rex Features*

Below: Enjoying the luxuries that weren't available in the Australian rainforest: pampering and, *right*, shopping with friend Michelle Heaton.

© *Icon Images/Rex Features*

Above left: A glum-looking Alex at Brisbane airport following Katie's post-jungle announcement that she no longer wanted to be with him. But that would change soon enough … *© Brian Cassey/Rex Features*

Above right: Back in England, Katie gets back to the business of promoting one of her books. *© Geoffrey Swaine/Rex Features*

Below: Presenting an award at the British Comedy Awards with Alan Carr and Jonathan Ross. *© Ken McKay/Rex Features*

Alex's moment of glory.
Above left: Departing for the *Celebrity Big Brother* house.

© *Solent News/Rex Features*

Above right and below: The champion! Alex emerges as the winner
of *Celebrity Big Brother* and is greeted by enthusiastic fans.

© *Channel 4/Rex Features; David Fisher/Rex Features*

Above: Katie and Alex return to the UK after their surprise wedding in Las Vegas.

Below: Katie shows off her amazing wedding ring.

Above left: Katie enjoys a spot of lunch at The Ivy in LA.

Above right: Looking fabulous at the VIP Style Awards with stylist
Lara Casey (*left*) and Michelle Heaton (*right*).

Below: Talking to Holly and Philip about her eventful life on
This Morning.

Above: Katie arrives in Vienna for the Vienna Opera Ball.

© *Karl Schoendorfer/Rex Features*

Below left: Making an entrance in a stunning blue ballgown.

© *Sipa Press/Rex Features*

Below right: With her hosts, Alexander Mayer, Irene Mayer and Prince Marcus von Anhalt.

© *Picture Perfect/Rex Features*

Promoting her hugely
popular reality TV show,
What Katie Did Next.
© *David Fisher/Rex Features*

Above: Even Katie and Alex weren't immune to ash-cloud delays. The couple embrace as they wait for their flight home at Sharm El Sheik airport.   © *Duncan Ridgley/Rex Features*

Below: At the Mixed Martial Arts Event in Birmingham – the pair had to endure being heckled by other members of the audience.

© *NTI Media Ltd/Rex Features*

helped out in the family business 'cos we owned a little beach resort back there. Those three months turned into three years, which was my stupid mistake. I basically had to take over the whole resort and redo it because mum and dad were sick, and we sent them home and me and my brothers took over.'

On another occasion he put this slightly differently, although the sentiment was still the same. 'Before I went into the jungle, my dad and I owned a beach resort in Australia near Brisbane,' he revealed. 'When I left the music industry in 2000, I went back and said to my parents that me and my brothers Mike, Chris, Danny and Andrew would take over the running of it, and they could go home and rest. I did that for two years without taking a wage. I asked my dad to let me learn how to live on nothing. I had my own business and a house in Australia that I had built, so I could have easily got a loan. It was hard for a couple of months. In a lot of ways I like to live quite simply. Yes, I do have a beautiful home in Cyprus, and dad and I like to sit outside and eat olives right from the tree, we do love the simple things. Making a conscious effort like that does make it easier to adapt your lifestyle if you're ever forced to.'

He was, of course, a very family oriented man and it was perfectly natural that before he had children of his own, he would want to help his parents out. It was also, however – although he might not have been able to admit it at the time – a way of coping with the loss of what had briefly been a stellar career. 'Well yeah, I had to do it 'cos it was our business and it wasn't fair that mum and dad had to run it,' he explained. 'They kept saying to me, "You've got to go back to England", and I was like, "No, I think it's good to have a break, people are probably sick of me." It was my stupidity.

'But after those three years I moved to New York and I wrote with some great people and I thought, my God, I have got some alright material – I could do it! So I spoke to my manager in England and she said, it's not the right time because of *Pop Idol* and all these different things that were out. So I went to Cyprus, opened up a little business and I thought I might just write for people, make a deal with the label, take it from there.'

The little business was a gym and many people were surprised to find someone who had only shortly beforehand been such a big star now running a small gym. Indeed, the *Cyprus Mail* tracked him down and demanded to know why he wasn't making music: 'I'm in negotiations now with record labels,' said Pete smoothly. And girlfriends? 'The special lady in my life is music. I haven't found the right lady that we would both want to be with each other the same amount.

Either she wants more and I don't, or I want more and she doesn't.' Why Cyprus? 'I love souvla, I love hanging on the balcony and just chilling out, having a coffee.' And there was the odd performance, including an anti-drugs awareness concert in Limassol. Still, it was a big break from the past.

And there matters might have stayed, were it not for a certain television show that put Pete right back in the limelight in a way that he would never have dreamed of at the time. It was in 2004 that he took the call that was to change his life, had he but known it, and introduce him to Kate. Not that he was very keen on the idea initially: in fact, he very nearly turned the whole thing down.

'Just at the time I was content and thought, I'm quite happy completely away from this industry, I got the call from *I'm A Celebrity*… And I had been called before for *Celebrity Big Brother* and *Celebrity Boxing*,' he confessed. Initially, the answer was no. 'I hate the phrase "turned them down" because it's as if you think you're too good for them,' he continued. 'It wasn't that, I just thought, what the hell am I gonna do in the *Big Brother* house? I thought I would get crucified, and I had this horrible feeling in my gut that I would make a fool of myself.'

In the event Pete never entered the *Big Brother* house, but he had registered with the production team.

Although the music industry had pretty much forgotten him, the makers of reality TV shows had not, not least because he made it clear that he might be interested if something else came along. 'I just didn't want to do it [*Celebrity Big Brother*],' he said. 'I said, "Please keep me in mind for other things" – and then *I'm A Celebrity...* came up.'

And so he agreed to appear – and in the process met the woman he was to marry, saw his career and public profile soar, and even managed to rise to some personal challenges, as well. 'Definitely, life changing in many ways,' he commented. 'Career-wise – definitely, relationship-wise – definitely, and I conquered my fears. You go to therapy for years to overcome some of your fears, y'know. And in two weeks, two of my three fears completely went. [They were] snakes and heights: spiders, I reckon about 70 per cent of the fear has gone. I can bear them now – I won't touch them, or talk to them. I came face to face with them twice, and I thought, well, if I can do that...' They did bite me in the glass tube and I did have to take antihistamines for two weeks – which no one knew about – I came out in a massive rash all over my back when I got bitten on my neck, but I faced my fears – that's huge.'

Far huger, however, was what happened next: Pete was not slow to take advantage of his new status –

'Mysterious Girl' was re-released in 2004, reaching number one, and so began a life of reality TV, possibly the most publicly-lived pop star life the world has ever seen. It was the way that Katie had lived for years, and so, reasoning would have had it, why shouldn't both of them let the cameras in the entire time? In the event, Pete was to feel that it was a mistake to live so very publicly, but hindsight is a great thing – back then, it all seemed perfectly sensible.

And his career was once more scaling the heights. After 'Mysterious Girl', he released 'Insania', which got to number three, followed by an album, *The Long Road Back*, although that didn't do so well, only reaching number 44. As he and Katie began to have children of their own, so they also began a musical collaboration: Pete's video for 'The Right Way' starred Katie and they also released an album of duets, *A Whole New World*, followed by a single of the same name, although neither went very far. In the meantime, of course, they scheduled in getting married before it all fell apart.

Post the split, Pete kept on working and in September 2009, he released 'Behind Closed Doors' from the album *Revelation*. It was clearly about the breakdown of his marriage – but at least Pete was able to use it for his art.

Pete used his second chance to good effect in other

ways, too. The last time he had been financially successful, he had not followed his father's advice but now, realising that this could be the chance to set himself up for life financially, he was far more astute.

'When I went to the jungle, he [Savvas] said, "If you go in there and anything comes out of it, and you don't invest, you will never get another chance again," Pete recalled. "You've had your chance and you're lucky you're getting a second chance in the industry. So I did: I built my house in Cyprus, I started investing in England and bought a couple of apartments. The thing is, when your money is tied up in property, you don't end up having much spare cash. I've been extravagant at times, but you have to learn to live on a lot less than you could live. Dad said that when you invest in property, you are setting up a future for your children. When you are young, you don't really understand that, but it's true – everything you build is for them.'

These days, he is proud of how sensible he has become. 'I think investing in things that bring in an income is preferable, as opposed to investing in something which might have capital gain,' he told one newspaper. 'Investing in that resort gave me an income each week (not as a salary, though) and I rent out my properties, which also brings in income. I don't mind talking about this, but for a long time it was, "Oh, Pete earns nothing" in the press. I used to get upset because I paid all my taxes and yet still got told I've got nothing. But my money was tied up in overseas properties – and doing so was one of the best decisions I ever made.'

Indeed, the days of recklessness were long gone and like any good Greek boy, he kept it in the family, employing his cousin as an accountant. The Pete of today knows that he was lucky to have had that second chance and he is determined to take full advantage of it.

The marriage itself eventually broke down in May 2009, but it hadn't been an easy ride in many other ways. For a start, while it might have made good television the couple's constant rowing was no way to lead a secure life. Both were jealous of the other: Pete didn't like Katie associating with the horsey set and something, clearly, was finally going to give. But before it did so, Pete suffered another bout of ill health when, in April 2007, he was diagnosed with a mystery illness, which turned out to be meningitis. It was a terrifying time – not least because a rumour had been racing around the Internet to the effect that he had actually died.

'I completely freaked out,' he admitted, a few years on. 'The thought that I could die from meningitis was in the back of my mind, but I certainly knew that I wasn't dead yet. It set my mind racing. Firstly, I worried that the doctors were not telling me something – that I was far more ill than they had led me to believe – and secondly, that my parents would have heard and been worried sick. I asked to speak to the doctor in charge of my case, who reassured me that if he had thought things were that serious, he would have had to tell me. So someone, possibly a hospital visitor or member of staff, must have started the rumour. But the psychological impact of hearing that I was supposed to be dead was something I would not wish on anyone.'

For someone given to panic attacks and the odd wobble, it must have been terrifying. But it was a serious illness, and although Pete made a complete recovery, it was a very frightening time. They had been in a hotel room in Los Angeles, he recalled, when suddenly it became apparent that something was very wrong.

'We'd had a really wonderful evening – instead of getting dressed up and going out for dinner, we decided to stay in with a bucket of Kentucky Fried Chicken,' said Pete. 'We ate the lot and then went to bed. But I woke up in the middle of the night, feeling very strange. The chicken kept repeating on me and I could taste the oil, which was making me feel very sick – or at least that's what I thought was making me feel sick. I also developed an odd headache at the back of my head. It felt as if something had hit me. However, I managed to get back to sleep eventually. When I woke up the following morning I didn't want to get out of bed.'

Any hopes this was just a bug that would blow over were dashed later that morning, when Pete began to feel increasingly ill. 'Kerrie-Ann, our stylist, had come to ask me if I wanted to go shopping with her before leaving for the airport, but there was no way I felt like going anywhere, let alone the shops,' he continued. 'I didn't have a temperature, but when I started coughing and the back of my head felt as though someone was hitting it hard, I knew this was not normal. I am someone who listens to what their body is trying to tell them and I knew that this was unlike anything I'd experienced before, but because it was hard to articulate exactly how I felt, Katie and Kerrie-Ann probably thought I was making a fuss and did mention the words "man flu".'

Pete was still not certain what was wrong, but managed to get to the airport and board the plane, although he was sick on numerous occasions throughout the flight. On arriving home he saw a doctor, who failed to realise what was wrong, the day after which Pete took matters into his own hands and asked Katie to call an ambulance, which took him to East Surrey Hospital.

'Katie seemed dubious about doing this, as the doctor had seemed unconcerned, but I insisted, "Get an ambulance now!"' he said. 'By the time the paramedics came – around an hour later – I was really panicking. I felt ready to pass out.' Once in situ, a large needle was placed in his body to drain the fluid: 'I found it horrible,' Pete continued. 'I was completely motionless and trying to smile through the pain, but tears were pouring out of my eyes and, at that point, I realised things could be serious. My doctor said that one strain [of meningitis] could be fatal, but not the other, and they didn't know which I had at that point. He added that I could be in hospital for 10 weeks, if it was the bacterial variety.'

Pete did what any typically Greek man would do: he got on the phone to his parents. But in those days Savvas was not in such good health – something that would later cause a big problem when Katie decided she didn't want the children to go to Australia. It was the only way they could see their paternal grandparent and Pete was very upset.

'I called my parents, Savvas and Thea in Australia where they live, but Dad had to get off the phone,' said Pete. 'He was in tears because the only other person he knew who'd had meningitis had died. Mum caught the first plane over, but had to leave Dad behind as he was unwell. She had never left him alone before so it was all rather traumatic. My older sister Debbie also came over. Mum cooked lots of food for me. She, Debbie and Katie – who had just six weeks to go before the birth of Princess Tiaamii – visited as much as possible.'

At this stage the marriage was still a happy one and Pete was able to take comfort from his wife. 'Katie was a great support, but I wouldn't let the kids come to the hospital with her – I didn't want them to see me like that and I was worried that they might catch something,' he admitted. Finally, they discovered that his meningitis was viral, rather than bacterial and thus less potentially dangerous, although he was not yet out of the woods.

'I was able to leave after two weeks to the day,' he recalled. 'I was walking very slowly and feeling most uncomfortable, but I was going home. I was weak, gaunt and had lost two stone. It may have been less serious than bacterial meningitis, but it was, nonetheless, a nasty experience that I wouldn't wish on anyone. The doctor's parting shot was, "Take it easy, Pete. Don't do anything for six or seven weeks." But I was determined to get fit and two weeks later, I was pumping iron in the gym we had in our house. Mind you, in truth it took six to 12 weeks for me to really get back to full strength. Sometimes Mum – who stayed with us until she was satisfied that all was okay – would go in the other room and cry because she couldn't bear to see me looking so awful. I can tell you that this episode really scared the life out of my parents.'

In the event, he returned to full health but it had been a very nasty experience, a health setback in a life that had been surprisingly full of such setbacks – surprising, because that is not the way that Pete comes across. But he is resilient, a fighter, and he has clawed his way back from more than one crisis in his life.

This, then, was the third person in the triangle. Very likeable, deeply family oriented, a man who has known the dizzying heights of success to be followed by the black depths of despair. Pete was the man Katie had believed to be her soul mate. And then it all went wrong.

Although it was Pete who finally left, however, he was also seen as the one who had been more of the victim in the relationship. But Pete is nothing if not a fighter, and it is a mistake to underestimate him as, perhaps, Katie had done. He had assessed the situation, decided it was time to move on – and was now building a brand new life for himself.

CHAPTER FIVE

OLD TENSIONS RESURFACE

So this, then, was the couple currently out in LA and the ex-husband back in the UK. Katie and Alex appeared remarkably unconcerned by all the publicity that was following them, and as for reports that their marriage wasn't legal – well, they simply laughed it off. 'Following the revelations in the press over the past couple of days regarding the validity of Katie and Alex's wedding, we would like to state that the marriage is 100 per cent legitimate and legal,' said their spokesman. 'The Wynn, where they married, and the Office of the County Clerk Marriage Services Division have both confirmed that Reverend Mose Henney, who conducted the wedding ceremony, is legally authorised to perform marriage ceremonies.'

Indeed, so unconcerned were they that they were snapped browsing first in a wig shop, and then in a sex shop, although there were some reports that Katie was still very upset following the news of Pete's fling. 'It was just unbelievable,' revealed a source. 'She was shouting at Pete and telling him what she thought of him as though she still has control over him. She was telling him that he's a liar. She said it would turn her career around again now that people knew what he's really like.'

Matters were shortly about to get a whole lot worse. Without realising it, Katie was making a rod for her own back: because it was so obviously possible to upset her where Pete was concerned, anyone who wanted to get a rise out of her simply had to find themselves supporting Pete. And that was exactly what was about to happen – from a very unexpected source.

But that was still to come. Back in Blighty, the mischievous journalist Piers Morgan was stirring it up again. He had compiled a list of the 100 celebrities who really matter, knowing full well that the celebrities left off the list would be livid that they hadn't made it, that the celebrities on the list would be livid that they weren't higher up – and at the same time he managed to capture the popular mood in an assessment of who mattered in celebrity land today.

Katie came in at 28, not bad given that the likes of Jude Law were way behind her, and Piers justified her inclusion in his own inimitable way.

'Why is she such a success? Simple,' he wrote. 'She is a beacon of hope for every young woman who dreams of being a star with large houses, flash cars, a footballer husband and a column in *Closer*. And who wants to do it the easy way, without any discernible trade, craft or art. I know Katie well, and like her a lot.' It was quite a compliment, coming from him.

Indeed, he had bumped into Katie when they were all in LA for the Oscars, an encounter he was only too happy to reproduce. 'I've come to cause a bit of chaos at the Oscars – what else?' Katie told him. 'In fact, I'm off to see my plastic surgeon now to have a load of Botox pumped into my face so I look great on Sunday. He did my boobs last time, but cocked it up and had to do them again.' Piers was clearly acting as Boswell to Katie's Samuel Johnson, a role he performed to perfection.

With perfect timing, Katie arrived back in the UK to provoke another paparazzi frenzy at the airport, while magnificently rising above it all. But still she couldn't break free of the drama surrounding Pete – and now another element of her past was to reappear in a way that was to cause her some aggravation. And so Kerry Katona entered the drama playing out in front of the nation, and very quickly became a central figure in it all, too.

Kerry Katona was, in fact, one of the few people in Britain who could rival Katie when it comes to acres of media coverage, garnering a similar level of fascination from the public, with a life that had in recent years been known to spin out of control. But like Katie, she possessed that indefinable quality that makes people empathise, that sense of a girl-next-door who hit the big time, and in Kerry's case, she very nearly lost it all. That the two women had actually once been friends just added further frisson to the situation: their fall-out accumulated mountains of media coverage. And now Kerry was linking up – albeit in friendship, at least – with Pete.

Kerry Jayne Elizabeth Katona was born on 6 September 1980 to the kind of background more often to be found in a misery memoir. She never knew her father and was brought up partly by her mother and partly by a succession of foster parents – four sets in all. There were times when she and her mother had to take shelter in a women's refuge. She attended eight different schools and witnessed dreadful violence in the home – her mother took up with a man called Dave Wheat, who Kerry witnessed attempting to stab Sue when she was just 13.

'All my life I'd been abandoned by people who were

meant to love me,' revealed Kerry later on. 'I still have no idea who my dad is. My mum chose her boyfriends over me every time, even though I so desperately wanted to be with her.'

Drink and drugs were present right from the start. Sue, herself the daughter of a prostitute, was an alcoholic: according to Kerry, she offered her drugs when she was still extremely young. She was just three years old when she saw Sue attempt to slit her wrists; on other occasions, she had to take her mother to hospital after an attempted overdose. 'I was 14 when my mum gave me speed – she told me it was sherbet,' she recalled. 'It wasn't unusual for my mum to do that, or for me to do drugs with my mum. It's normal where I grew up.'

After Wheat, who had been imprisoned for murder, died in a car crash, Sue sank into such depression that she tried to kill herself – the young Kerry was once forced to hand her a bottle of pills – while her own suffering can hardly be imagined. 'The saddest thing was, I was actually a really good little kid,' Kerry admitted sadly, some years later. 'People look at care kids and think they are a bad lot – I always wanted to be neat and tidy for school and to be this little angel.'

But that was soon knocked out of her. When she was 16, Kerry left school to become a lapdancer, during which time she posed for a set of glamour shots – almost inevitably, these resurfaced when she became famous. And famous she was. Despite the nightmarish past she had emerged from, Kerry hit the big time very early on, when aged 18, she became a member of the pop group Atomic Kitten. They really hit the stratosphere shortly after she left, but the association was enough to get her on her way.

Kerry left the band because she was pregnant by the man she would go on to marry, Brian McFadden (and relations between them would one day make Katie and Pete's post-divorce relationship look like Romeo and Juliet). She moved to find work in television, making a great success of it, and appeared on shows such as *Loose Women* and *Elimidate*, a cross between a reality show and a dating show. In fact, she had a natural air about her that made viewers relate to her (her dreadful childhood was not publicly known at the time although even when the news finally did come out, it only served to warm the public towards her rather than anything else), and all this would lead to a very successful career in reality TV. But in later years, Kerry's life was to veer massively off the rails and it was her efforts to get herself back on track again and recreate the success she'd once had that made her link forces with Pete.

She was, in many ways, a force to be reckoned with, which Katie appeared not to understand. Her awful childhood had given her an inner strength that she would need when things went wrong for her as an adult: she ended up with one husband, Brian, who frolicked with a lapdancer just before the wedding before leaving her for someone else, and a second husband with whom things did not turn out as she had hoped. Kerry allowed herself to be pushed about by men in a way that would have been inconceivable for Katie (she might have had her man problems, but she certainly never let any of them take advantage of her), but at the bottom of it all was a core of steel. She was a fighter, and when she finally hit rock bottom, she was determined to fight back.

Kerry's growing television career was really taking off when the pair first became acquainted. Katie and Kerry met back in the celebrity jungle in 2004 – indeed, Kerry, at the time married to Brian McFadden, had gone on to win the show. During the time in the jungle, she became a sort of go-between and confidante for Katie and Pete: she listened to their doubts about what was happening, issued gentle encouragement and generally tried to help them both get it on. The growing romance really roused the nation's interest, sowing the first seeds of fascination with the story that was to become Katie and Pete, but Kerry held her own as well. At the time, no one involved could have guessed that one day, after Katie and Pete had married, created a family and then divorced, Kerry and Katie would be at complete loggerheads – and that Kerry would take Pete's side.

In the aftermath of the jungle, Katie and Kerry remained friends. It was not hard to see why: they were both tough, both survivors, both accustomed to living in the public eye and both used to taking a modicum of talent and turning it into a hugely successful long-term career. When Katie and Pete got married in 2005, Kerry was one of the bridesmaids. But then it all seemed to go wrong.

Kerry and Brian's marriage did not survive. Under the nation's gaze Kerry very visibly fell apart, eventually spending time in The Priory, before embarking on a second, disastrous marriage: to a local cab driver, Mark Croft in 2007. This, too, would ultimately end in divorce (much to the relief of those who knew and cared about her), but in the early days, it also proved the catalyst for the end of Katie and Kerry's friendship. Katie publicly voiced what an awful lot of people were thinking, namely that Mark seemed to be bad news, with the result that the two fell out.

Of course, this had been forgotten by the time that Katie and Pete's own divorce came through by all but those immediately involved and so it must have stirred up a few emotions when Kerry and Mark finally split up in 2010. Almost immediately afterwards, she signed up with a new manager, Claire Powell of Can Associates. 'Kerry knows this is her last chance,' said Claire. 'There will be no drugs and no Mark. She has signed a legal document agreeing to that. Kerry approached me six months ago to take her on, but I refused while Mark was still around. I do not believe he has been a positive influence on her. If she is prepared to work hard and stay clean, she has a great career ahead of her.'

What made the news notable was the fact that Claire was also Pete's manager – and had been Katie's, too, until she and Pete split the previous year. Kerry now started to turn up at Pete's concerts – entirely innocently, of course, as it was just a case that the two had the same manager. But tongues began to wag and the entirely false gossip began that there was perhaps a romantic relationship between them. In a very off way, it would seem to make sense.

Over the next few weeks, Kerry and Pete were continually spotted chatting together or supporting one another in their various endeavours. If nothing else, it made good marketing sense.

It must be said that in the immediate wake of Kerry's split from Mark, Katie's reaction was unhelpful, boiling down as it did to, 'I told you so.' 'I told her years ago that I didn't trust Mark and that I thought he was a bully and I meant it,' she declared. 'It's just a shame she didn't believe me – I was only trying to be a friend. It's down to her what she does, but it's just like a man who hits a woman. They go back crying, apologising and begging, and convince their partners to give them a second chance, but they end up doing it again.'

That, however, was before the new friendship with Pete began (and it would hardly have put Kerry off joining Team Pete). And when Kerry and Pete suddenly appeared to become each other's new best mate from nowhere, Katie didn't seem to know what to think. Indeed, her thoughts veered wildly from day to day. To begin with, she actually appeared to encourage the rumours that Pete and Kerry had become close, although she would very soon change her mind about that one.

'Katie really believes Kerry has got the hots for Pete,' revealed a source close to her. 'And now they have the same agent it is only a matter of time before they realise they are right for each other. Kerry is already close to Peter – he has been a great support since she signed up with the Can Associates agency. Now that Katie is happy with Alex Reid, she would actually love to see Peter and Kerry get it on together.'

That was highly unlikely. For a woman as competitive as Katie, chances are that she would have been pretty down on whoever Pete got together with in the wake of their break-up, and given that Kerry was actually present in the jungle when Katie and Pete became close, there was almost no chance at all that she'd welcome such a union. What is far more likely was that Katie was preparing herself in public for the eventuality of Kerry and Pete getting together, in case she might one day have to put a brave face on it. Her tone was to change quite significantly, not least when it became increasingly apparent that none of the stories were true.

Indeed, if Katie was upset by this turn in events, she wasn't showing it. Never one to take these things lying down, friends began to suspect that she was preparing to launch a counter offensive, as only she knew how – by befriending Kerry once more, thus placing herself squarely in the middle of the enemy camp. After all, if she and Kerry became friends, it would make it even more difficult for Kerry and Pete to be a couple, to say nothing of stirring things up for Claire, as well.

'If there's one woman you should never cross, it's Katie,' said a source. 'She really knows how to get to people. She's only too aware that it would freak out her former manager Claire Powell – who looks after both Peter and Kerry – if she were to befriend Kerry again. She also says that would put the spotlight back on her. She's barely keeping her anger in check at the moment, but she's developing a plan for huge success this year that'll blow Pete and Kerry out of the water.'

Whether Katie would succeed in her plan is debatable, however, not least because Kerry and Pete seemed pretty determined to look after each other. Pete publicly told the world that Kerry had a 'good heart'; Kerry returned the compliment by announcing that she was on 'Team Pete', adding for good measure that Katie had behaved badly. If they were trying to make it clear that it was the two of them against her, they could hardly have done better. And they had something else in common, too: both felt they had been treated badly by Katie, Kerry because Katie had badmouthed Mark, and Pete in the wake of the marriage breaking down.

Kerry and Pete, of course, were fully aware that what they were doing was fanning the flames. 'I remember seeing a clip of Katie kick off at Pete and it was disgusting,' said Kerry. 'I wouldn't have stood for it. I love Pete, I'm Team Pete all the way. Pete's the best thing that ever happened to her. She's walked all over him and he just looks so sad. She totally crucified him on a TV show talking about his bollocks – I'm not surprised that he ended up leaving her.' It was incendiary stuff. Shortly afterwards, Kerry also signed a deal to do a reality TV show.

Katie was completely bemused. 'I don't know what Pete thinks he's playing at, she's just a poor man's version of me,' she is said to have told a friend. 'He's making a fool of himself and she is a total disgrace for doing this to a mate.'

Her other friends felt the same: 'She knows they're with the same management and thinks it's just a PR stunt,' said one.

But Kerry didn't think they were mates at all. Given that she had spent her entire life being let down by those closest to her – first, her mother and then her two husbands – she was more than used to the vagaries of fortune, of thinking you'd found someone you could trust and then learning you could do nothing of the sort. That didn't mean she liked it, though. If there was anyone in the world who needed a really good, solid friendship, it was Kerry Katona, but she certainly hadn't found it with Katie. Was it any wonder that she was clearly hoping she might at last find the friend she needed in Pete?

A picture of Kerry and Pete together appeared on the cover of *OK!* magazine. This gave rise to even more speculation about the two – a joint appearance on the front page of a celebrity journal being tantamount to an engagement announcement – but it turned out to be a false alarm. It was not what it seemed, as Pete made clear on his Twitter page.

'Sorry to disappoint anyone who wants to know, but one million per cent not true about Kerry Katona, sweet girl though,' he tweeted. 'Photos in OK were mock-up.'

In case that wasn't enough (and already annoyed about being linked to a huge variety of women since the split from Katie), Pete went one step further and made it absolutely clear what the real nature of the relationship was. 'There was a story in one of the tabloids and a magazine last week that said Kerry and I are in love. There is no truth in this at all,' he wrote in *Now* magazine. 'She actually said she loves me as a friend and that was said a long time ago. We have been mates for a long time, but since she has signed to my management, I have seen her twice. She came along to two gigs, but we have not been out for cosy dinners and we are definitely not a couple. There is absolutely no way in the world I would cross that line with Kerry.'

Given Kerry's own unfortunate history of romantic relationships, it was probably just as well.

But while Pete might have been canny enough to realise that, much as he liked her, Kerry was probably not the ideal woman with whom to link up, the friendship they were giving one another was a source of strength to them both – and the resulting publicity wasn't harming either of their newly regenerated careers. Kerry and Pete were not linked romantically, but they were doing one another no end of good in just about every other way. The public seemed to like it, too.

Just as Kerry was happy to stand up for Pete, however, so Katie found supporters in her hour of need as well. The singer Boy George, who had also spoken out in support of Alex, was determined to make it clear that Katie was a very different person in real life from the slightly negative image she sometimes portrayed. 'I've met Katie a few times,' he said. 'She's been to my house and I find her sweet as hell. She's not a nasty person. She doesn't always do herself justice on TV, but I think as a person she's actually quite sweet and I don't understand why people hate her.'

It was certainly true, however, that Katie and Alex provoked very strong emotions and there was sometimes a danger this could get out of hand. In late March the pair of them attended a nightclub together, but were turned on by a drunken mob in scenes that could very easily have got out of hand. They became separated in the scrum, with Katie screaming out for Alex, and it was only when security guards stepped in that she was able to get back to her car. Alex joined her soon afterwards: both were clearly extremely shaken.

'Kate and Alex just wanted to have as quiet a night as possible, but it's always bedlam when they're together,' said a witness to the scene. 'They are not doing anything unusual, but it does get heated from time to time. Kate only has one security guard at the moment and she knows the staff at Mo*vida well, so they all pitch in and help her get in and out. But now Alex is on the scene that may not be enough.'

Indeed, there seemed to be a real need to bump up security around the couple. They could scarcely walk down the street without causing a riot – the attention was as great as anything Katie had experienced with Pete.

At least this proved that they were still ahead in the publicity stakes, however. Kerry and Pete might have managed to make the pages of the newspapers and magazines when they praised each other or when Kerry turned up at one of his concerts, which she increasingly frequently did, but they certainly weren't capable of causing a riot in the streets. Nor, in the unlikely event of their actually getting together, did they look to be in the same league as Katie and Alex. People were fascinated, but not in quite the same shape-shifting way as they were with Katie and her new beau, whose antics continued to dominate the press.

But there was a downside to it all, too. The attention

was also taking its toll on Alex, at least. You had to be a certain type of person to deal with all the attention and still stay sane – Alex had to learn fast. Katie had been famous ever since she was a teenager and so she was accustomed to dealing with the scrum, even if it did sometimes get out of hand, but Alex was not. His fight with Tom Watson was coming up – indeed, he had been filming the training for his reality TV show, *The Fight Of His Life*, but now there were fears that his new life had been taking up so much of his time that he simply hadn't put in the training and pulling out was a consideration.

'Alex is so worried about the fight he's even wondered if he could cancel or postpone it,' said a source close to the couple. 'It would be tough, even if he was at his career best, but he's had less time for training than he'd like because of new work commitments.' Indeed, his life had been turned upside down. It was also clear this was a chance to do what he had wanted to do all those years ago, for fighting was, it should be remembered, his second choice of career, not his first. His fighting might have suffered through all of this, but if he did want to go back to acting, it wasn't exactly doing him any harm.

In public, life went on as normal. Katie appeared at the Mark Price VIP Style Awards in Dublin, an event often referred to as the 'Irish Style Oscars': wearing a very mini, miniskirt, as ever, she stood out from the crowd. But matters took a turn for the bizarre, when reports surfaced that she wanted to move house because she thought her own home might be haunted. The trouble seemed to have started the previous year when the TV psychic Sally Morgan had visited the house and claimed to have felt a presence.

'Katie wants out of there quickly as she's convinced it's haunted by a pair of ghosts,' said a source. 'She feels like she's being driven out of her own home by spirits – she's had enough. Even Alex has told her he's seen the ghost. They're convinced there's an old lady upstairs; you can't tell them otherwise. Katie has a sun-bed room near the bottom of the house and she believes it's haunted by a ghost.'

A sun-bed room would certainly not be everyone's idea of a place visited by ghostly presences – but then this was Katie Price.

Even when she was garnering attention in other activities, however, the spectre of Kerry and Pete continued to loom large. The fact that Pete was still sometimes on Katie's mind was in evidence when she appeared on *This Morning* to tell Phillip Schofield and Holly Willoughby that she and Alex would be holding a second wedding ceremony in the summer and inadvertently used the phrase, 'mine and Pete,' before hastily correcting it to, 'I mean, mine and

Alex...' Who could blame her? The new relationship had all happened in a considerable rush – and it's a mistake many people with new partners in their lives have made.

Of course, this caused uproar. Cynics had been looking for a reason to say that Katie had never got over Pete, that she had married Alex only on the rebound or as a publicity stunt, that the relationship wouldn't last – anything they could think of to try and make people think that Katie had not, as she so often said she had, moved on. And to call her new husband by the name of the old one, that was an embarrassment indeed, according to the press.

Katie recovered from it quickly – she always did. She was happy enough, though, to talk about the upcoming happy event, in the form of the next set of nuptials, the planning of which was already underway. 'Well, because our family couldn't be there and the reason we got married in Vegas was because Alex proposed to me after his first fight – my first fight of seeing him – in September and we tried to get married at Christmas,' she explained. 'And the only place we could get married was Vegas because you have to be divorced a certain amount of time to get married here, abroad, anywhere so Vegas was the only place to go. We are doing like a blessing in the summer because we want all our family there. His mum would like to see her son get married and my mum would like to see it again so yeah, we can't wait.'

According to Katie, this would be a far more private occasion than the nuptials with Pete, which involved a huge pink wedding dress, glass coach and the works, however. 'We are both going to decide together and get our families involved – his mum, my mum, we're all going to do it as a family thing – how really it should be done, not how other people tell you to do it,' she continued. 'We're not going to have a wedding planner; we're literally going to do it ourselves.'

She was also very keen to add to her family with her new husband. 'His fighter name is Reidinator, so you know when you say pregnated so like I've been Reidinated!' she exclaimed. 'So we are trying for a baby. I can't wait. Yeah, I can't wait!' This was to become something of a theme over the next few weeks: Katie and Alex constantly fuelled speculation that she was pregnant before it emerged that actually, she wasn't. Both were clearly keen to get started, though, and a baby would at last silence those doubters.

It was, however, a high-risk strategy to talk so publicly about their hopes. Sometimes it is easy to forget when a couple have such a high profile that it's actually real people behind the glamour, with all the hopes and fears that entails. The more they talked about wanting to have a baby together, the more it reminded everyone that they hadn't actually got one – and that risked building up a pressure of its own.

It's well known that couples sometimes have a problem in conceiving even when there are no actual medical problems, because psychologically there is a barrier. That certainly wasn't their intention, but it was hard to escape the conclusion that Katie and Alex were being a little premature in not thinking this one through. But Katie had never had any problems before in conceiving. Why should she now?

CHAPTER SIX

KATIE SPEAKS OUT

It had been good for Katie to appear on *This Morning*, however, for a great deal of criticism had been recently levelled against her and this was a chance, once and for all, to make it clear what lay behind some of her actions. She used the occasion to address some of the more controversial charges. Princess had been pictured wearing make-up, which drew some angry comments from Pete and raised eyebrows elsewhere. Katie was as defiant as ever, not least because she was launching her own cosmetic range for the very young.

'I'm doing children's make-up and Princess isn't the face or fronting it,' she explained. 'We went to Disneyland a few weeks ago and they do make-up there [that has] glitter in it, but mine won't be having glitter, it'll be no different to what they sell at Toys R Us – it'll be edible and safe.' And as for Princess: 'The amount of times I go to get my lip liner and it's blunt because she's there, trying it on or drawing on the mirror with it, but that's just a child. All my friends' daughters do it.' And with a mother who loved make-up as much as Katie, Princess was almost bound to want to give it a go.

The children continued to be a flashpoint, however. It could not have been much fun for Pete to watch another man enter their lives; whilst there was the occasional outburst about make-up or hair straighteners, he had been careful never to speak out against Alex. Indeed, the only overt concern he'd ever shown had been when the cross-dressing stories broke, and even then he was careful that he never said too much. It would have made it more difficult for the children themselves, of course, if Pete had publicly had a go at Alex. Whatever he might think about it, Alex's role was as a father figure and it made sense to respect that.

But Katie was a different matter. Pete could barely contain himself when it came to his ex. It took nothing to rile him: not just Princess's hair and make-up, but his (understandable) anger when Katie began raising her voice to him down the phone when Junior was there. This, in many ways, would have been the most painful part of the separation for a family man like Pete: clearly, he adored his children and the fact that he was so estranged from their mother was a big problem for them all, yet he didn't want to make matters even worse.

That there was still a good deal between them, though, was evident – and there probably always would be. It is sometimes forgotten that although Katie was doing very well as a model when they first met, while Pete's music career seemed to be well behind him, Katie was actually not faring quite so well as previously. Indeed, it was beginning to look as if hers would be one of those careers you come across all too often: a brief spell as a glamour model in her late teens and early twenties, followed by oblivion. The fact that it hadn't happened – in fact, her career soared after leaving the jungle – had a huge amount to do with her union with Pete. He saved her just as much as she saved him: and that shared history, the fact that they'd got one another's careers going again, wasn't going to go away.

In some ways, it was hardly surprising that Katie inadvertently called Alex, Pete. That mix-up with the names, though, had been embarrassing and Alex was very keen to ensure that everyone knew he wasn't bothered by it at all. According to him, it was the kind of thing that could have happened to anyone.

'When Katie said: "Me and Pete" on *This Morning*, I didn't have a problem with it at all,' he revealed. 'Slip-ups happen. I've called ex-girlfriends the wrong name before, or I've called Katie my girlfriend when she's my wife. She was talking about Pete just before, so it is ridiculous to make a big deal of it. I do get jealous – I'm human – but that moment hasn't made me insecure in the slightest. I know how strong we are as a couple.'

Given the publicity surrounding them, however, it was inevitable that people would talk – and talk they did. Indeed, behind the scenes was speculation that although Alex was laughing it off in public, in private it was quite another matter. It seemed that this was not the first time it had happened and he was becoming increasingly fed up.

'It's not the first time she's said "Pete" instead of "Alex",' said a source. She says it's just a slip of the tongue, but it makes Alex furious ...'

Of course, there had been positive elements to her relationship with Pete, too. The father of Katie's first child – Dwight Yorke – had not stuck around, something that would have tested any mother, no matter how strong they were, whereas Pete willingly took on the paternal role with Harvey, not just with his own children, Junior and Princess. To think that you have found love and lost it is devastating enough, but when the person involved has also assumed fatherly duties when he didn't need to do so is worse still. And whatever everyone else was saying, it was still incredibly early days. The fact was that Katie and Pete hadn't been separated for a year, much less divorced.

In the immediate aftermath of the break-up, Katie had unwisely gone on the *Graham Norton Show* and alleged that Pete was having an affair with his manager Claire Powell: the remarks had not actually been broadcast, but made in front of the audience and fellow guests.

Both Pete and Claire had been incandescent about the claims: Pete because he and Claire were old friends who had a strictly professional relationship and also because it implied that he was a hypocrite after very publicly stating that he intended to remain celibate until he was divorced; and Claire because she was living with her fiancé Neville Hendricks. Indeed, both felt so strongly that the matter had gone to court and in mid-March blew up in Katie's face. She was forced to apologise unreservedly and pay 'substantial' undisclosed compensation. In her hurt following the breakdown of the marriage, of course, she had lashed out wildly at everyone but this time she really might just have gone too far.

Indeed, Claire had been very upset by the whole

episode. 'To be accused of infidelity, with one of her long-standing and high-profile clients, was obviously very damaging and distressing for Ms Powell – the most obvious reason being that the allegation was completely untrue,' her solicitor Mike Brookes told the High Court.

'It was just a lie,' said Claire after the hearing. 'But it upset me, it upset my fiancé and it upset Pete. I'm just glad it's been sorted. I didn't really want to be in court, but if something bad is said which is going to trash your reputation, you have to clear your name.'

Katie herself, recognising that this time she really had gone too far, was contrite. 'She greatly regrets what has happened and joins in the making of this statement in order to assist setting the record straight,' stated her lawyer, Keith Ashby. But then it might also have been the case that Katie couldn't believe that Pete would end the marriage if he didn't already have another woman on the sidelines. She herself usually had a man in tow, and so she assumed the same about Pete. But by now it was evident that, quick flings or not, Pete was determined to hold out until he found someone he really did want to be serious with – and he certainly hadn't found her yet.

Pete, meanwhile, had his own take on the state of play. Katie had made a big song and dance about having a tattoo with his name on her wrist removed;

Pete had said that for the sake of the children, his own tattoo – on his ring finger – would stay. However, he appeared to have changed his mind. Katie was, after all, now married to someone else and so he appeared in public with a plaster over the finger in question. It seemed he was having his tattoo lasered off after all, in a symbolic gesture, as well as a physical one. The past was being erased; Pete was once more becoming his own man.

There was certainly no love lost between Katie and Claire these days. It was Claire who had originally been credited with transforming her image from Jordan the glamour girl to Katie Price, devoted mother and businesswoman. The sudden and abrupt return of Jordan the previous summer might well have been an indication of what had gone wrong. Neither Katie nor Claire had ever given the real reason behind their split or who had instigated it. Indeed, in the immediate aftermath of the parting, Claire seemed very sad at the turn of events. 'We were close friends,' she said at the time. 'I thought I would be doing her branding going into her fifties. [But] Katie loves being Jordan, and she may have thought, I want to be Jordan, but you are forcing me to be Katie.'

Katie went further than that. The tensions with Claire had started years earlier, well before the split from Pete, and she openly blamed Claire for being responsible for what happened. 'The trouble is, before, I felt married to two people – Pete and our management,' she said in November 2009, in remarks that were not meant to imply an affair – merely a very suffocating relationship. 'And it was like Pete was married to two women, Claire and me. And it just suffocated me. If I'm going to blame anyone for the end of my relationship with Pete, I'd have to lay some of the blame with Claire.'

Surprisingly, Claire actually appeared to agree. 'Yes, I did have to control Kate to a certain extent, as can be seen since she stopped being my client,' she said, somewhat wryly. 'Pete doesn't need to be controlled like Kate. None of my other clients do, it was only her.'

It was a strange echo of Princess Diana's remark that there had been, 'three of us in this marriage,' especially given the importance Katie attached to her career. But perhaps, without even necessarily acknowledging it herself, Katie had felt the constant encroachment of the television cameras to be at times a little wearisome. Her career had become her life and vice versa: the line too blurred.

Then again, there was also the fact that the two women simply wanted Katie's career to go in different directions, with Katie wishing for a return to her earlier days. When Katie originally parted from

Claire's management there had been a good deal of speculation as to how it was going to affect her career. The answer seemed to be that it wasn't impacting in the slightest: apart from being constantly in the limelight, Katie continued to endorse a huge range of products and was now even being spoken of as a potential guest star on the Australian soap, *Neighbours*. (That Pete had been brought up in Australia must have added certain piquancy to the whole mêlée.)

'The guys on Ramsay Street are keen to get her on for a one-off,' said a source. 'Like Lily Allen last year – who knows, Katie and Alex could be the new Kylie and Jason.'

Back in the UK, she had launched her children's sporting range of clothing, KP Equestrian, and raised eyebrows when Junior and Princess were pictured modelling the clothes on the website. Originally Katie had said that she would not be using them, but in the event, they appeared after all. 'This wasn't planned and came about as the children played with their mum,' Katie's spokesman said, as the inevitable furore began. 'They saw her modelling and wanted to have a go. It was something they enjoyed very much and was good family fun.'

And Katie rose above it all. Not only was she not bothered about what people were saying about her children with Pete, but she was still trying her hardest to start a new family with Alex, too. She was also spending time doing what she liked best – namely, riding – but even here, her life was not without incident. It seemed that whatever she did, there was some drama and the latest occurred when she was out on horseback with her friend and stylist, Melodie Pope. Melodie was thrown from the horse, although thankfully Katie was there to help.

'Katie was shocked when she turned around to see her friend hurled on the ground in a heap,' said a friend. 'It was a very nasty fall but she didn't panic, not even seeing how much pain her friend was in. She just calmly called the emergency services and arranged for paramedics to come and help Melodie. Katie cleared her diary for the afternoon to be by Melodie's side until doctors told her Melodie was in a stable condition. The pair were having such a lovely day, riding near Katie's home, until Melodie was injured. She suffered excruciating lower-back injuries.'

Strictly speaking, this was Melodie's drama rather than Katie's, but it was indicative of a life that seemed in perpetual motion, with no chance ever to calm down and smell the roses. Frenetic activity was the order of the day. If she wasn't launching children's ranges of equestrian wear here, she was filming her reality TV show there, punctuated by numerous other endorsements, appearances, dramas, public fights with Pete, angry spats with anyone else who upset her, and in the background, the ongoing relationship with Alex Reid. And how was that going? The two talked as enthusiastically about each other as ever: both were adamant they'd found true love.

Behind the scenes, however, there were reports that she was becoming agitated that she was not already pregnant – not least because she'd never had a problem conceiving before. Having spoken about it so openly added to the weight of expectation, of course, but it was not in Katie's nature to do anything privately. If she and Alex were trying for a baby, then the whole world would know about it. It's just that when the baby failed to appear, there was a great deal of speculation about why not.

Alex, easy-going fellow that he was, was happy to laugh off the more outlandish of the rumours about how hard they were trying for a child. 'Three times a day? I wish!' he wrote in his *Star* magazine column. 'We do have to work, you know! I like to keep things like that private, but some days we don't even do it at all. Getting pregnant is on our to-do list, but for now we're just enjoying each other. When it does happen, I'll be the happiest man on earth and will shout it from the rooftops!'

What a hostage to fortune it was, and Katie was

also being far too open about something that had not yet happened, not that she wasn't trying her best: 'Katie will be 32 in May and she's been advised it may not be as easy to get pregnant as it was in the past, if she doesn't take care of herself,' revealed a source. 'She's been eating a diet high in iron, which means lots of red meat, seafood and leafy greens, such as spinach. It's the reason she's put on a few pounds recently. A month ago, her diet consisted mostly of biscuits and handfuls of snacks when she got hungry.

'Her new diet is causing rows because Alex is training for an important fight and he's on the "caveman diet", which is totally different from what she wants him to eat. Alex usually does what Katie says, but when he's training he can be very stubborn and single-minded. Katie keeps making snide remarks about his fighting and she's blown her top a couple of times. She wants Alex to stay at home and be a house husband, so she gets irritated that he takes his career so seriously.'

It was a mistake she'd made before. Tensions came to a head with Pete because Katie had been competitive with him, determined to be the top dog, and unsurprisingly, Pete hadn't liked it. Moreover, Alex himself appeared to want to keep his own career going. He clearly accepted that he was very much in

Katie's shadow but still wanted to do something under his own name, too.

But being part of the Katie Show took up a lot of time. The couple had decided to stage a second set of nuptials in the summer and had done a deal for Katie's reality TV show: they were to be paid £600,000 for the rights, to be shown on ITV2's *What Katie Did Next: Wedding Special*. Despite the plans, however, there were still reports about tensions behind the scenes. To live so constantly in the public glare was bound to bring difficulties with it – and it had certainly done so with Pete – and there were rumours of trouble in paradise, despite the fact that they had been married less than two months. Katie's continuing failure to become pregnant seemed to be the problem, along with Alex's ongoing career.

Said a source, 'Katie's the sort of girl who needs excitement in a relationship, but she's showing signs of frustration and boredom. She thinks what she needs more than anything is another baby – she's desperately broody and is telling people she's at the stage where she might have to give up. She's turning getting pregnant into a military operation – calling it the "Reidination Project". She is even demanding he give up his career as a fighter to concentrate on building a family.'

This was all very well, but Alex was being held

responsible for something he could not control. What's more, it had ominous echoes of yesteryear: Katie demanding that she alone should run the show, while at the same time putting Alex down. It was far from clear if there was a genuine problem when it came to conceiving – since the marriage, the pair had spent a fair amount of time apart – and if there was, it was equally unclear whose problem it was. Sometimes, it seemed as if Katie couldn't resist humiliating her menfolk in the area designed to hurt most: she had, after all, very publicly described Peter Andre's accoutrements as being like 'an acorn' (something his other conquests were only too happy to repudiate).

While it would be going too far to say that Katie had deliberately attempted to announce her pregnancy to coincide with launching her new babyware range, the fact was that she had far too often in the past allowed her private life to become mixed up with her professional one. If she did see the marriage to Alex as just another platform from which to market her life-as-career, then the union could well be doomed.

And the lack of a child appeared to be making matters worse. In Katie's eyes, bizarre as it may sound, this would also be seen as one up for Pete. Katie appeared to think that everything in her life heralded some form of competition with her ex-husband and if she'd publicly stated that she wanted to get pregnant by another man and it failed to happen, while she'd had no problem in bearing his children, would that not prove that the second marriage was not so fulfilling as the first? It's not the way most people would have thought, but then Katie wasn't most people: she wanted a baby and she wasn't getting pregnant – ergo, someone else was to blame.

Pete himself was very wisely staying out of it – and besides, he had other fish to fry. He would be appearing regularly on a new chat show on Channel 4, *The 5 O'Clock Show*, and guess who was planning to make a guest appearance? Kerry was one of the first people he approached, alongside *X-Factor* winner, Alexandra Burke, in a way that did not look like pleasing his ex. Not that Pete was concerned: it was potentially a whole new string to his bow. 'This is very much being seen as a trial for Pete,' said a friend. 'He is keen to impress as the door is wide open for him to secure a permanent deal. If he manages to get great guests, then it will help his cause massively.'

Indeed, and it looked like a good move. Pete was well aware of the vagaries of the music industry – after all, he'd seen his career disappear before – and this time around, he was determined to plan ahead, should something similar occur. There was another, more obvious reason for expanding his horizons as well: he wanted to stay in the UK. Last time he'd had a career flux, there had been nothing and no one to stop him from going back to Cyprus to lick his wounds. But this time around, he had Junior and Princess, plus Harvey, and wanted to develop a career that would allow him to stay close to them all.

Meanwhile, what of Katie and Alex? If some people were to be believed, matters were actually far worse behind the scenes than it appeared – there was even talk in the press of the marriage being on the rocks. 'They're being urged to go to counselling sessions because Katie hates the thought of being twice-divorced,' continued the source. 'But they're at each other's throats, day and night. They don't have explosive rows – it's more simmering contempt, sniping and little hurtful comments that eat away at their marriage. Alex is hurt that what is meant to be a loving, natural process is now all about fitting it in with her diary.' None of this speculation has ever been commented on by Katie or Alex.

Then there was the issue of his name, or rather, the fact that his new wife continued to call him by the name belonging to her ex-husband. 'He said if Katie calls him Pete one more time he's going to start calling her by his exes' names,' said the source. 'Katie is always saying horrible things to him or stuff that hurts him. Alex said, "She's bossy. I don't know why she does that – she tries to reject me, then panics as I will walk."' Was history repeating itself? It was exactly as Pete had reacted.

Despite the constant warring with his former wife, Pete was also looking on with some concern. Whatever he might feel about Katie personally, she was, after all, the mother of his children; if she was unhappy, it would impact on them. Pete was becoming increasingly concerned that she was, 'desperately unhappy and acting erratically,' revealed a source. 'Despite everything, she's his children's mum; he genuinely wants her to be okay. He's a huge advocate of therapy, he knows how bad things can get.'

Of course, Pete had had difficulties with depression and anxiety in the past as indeed, had Katie – and so he knew what he was talking about. But it was inconceivable that Katie would undergo any kind of therapy, not least because this would entail admitting that something was actually wrong. No one was better at putting on a brave face in public than Katie, and the chances of her admitting to any doubts at all about her current situation were nil.

It was hard not to feel for Alex, however, who could not have begun to understand the exact nature of the drama he was walking into, for the very good reason that no one other than Katie and Pete would know what it was like to be at the centre of such a maelstrom. After all, they had spent years creating it and learning to live within it and so they knew what life in the spotlight was really like.

But Alex didn't, and while he clearly saw the many advantages it held – his future prospects were looking up – the downside was not inconsiderable as well. Whatever the truth about what was going on behind the scenes, in the space of a few days he'd had to put up with rumours that Katie was unimpressed by his low sperm count (not that anyone knew whether this really was the case), wanted to make him look more like Pete, frequently called him Pete and was eager for him to give up his career as a fighter. It was a lot for anyone to take on board.

But what it was easy for the cynics to overlook was that Alex clearly loved Katie – as indeed, had Pete. The fact that they lived so publicly didn't mean that the emotions they felt were any less real – indeed, anyone seeing Katie's gaunt appearance in the immediate aftermath of Pete's departure couldn't have failed to realise just how devastated she was – and the fact is, Alex was not with Katie for the publicity. He was with Katie for Katie, and even if the circumstances of their marriage had been a little unusual, he was determined to finish what he'd started. After all, they were now man and wife.

And so this strange dance that had at first existed as a trio now turned into a quartet. Alex was fast learning about his new life, while Katie created drama everywhere she turned. Effortlessly the centre of attention, she appeared to have designs on becoming the most famous woman in the world. Pete continued to be the doting father as he worried about his children, built up his career and started to wonder if the time was finally right to have a new girlfriend.

Meanwhile, Kerry Katona revelled in her newfound freedom and her new career, her friendship with Pete and what lay ahead. Now she had become part of their story – and she wasn't about to go away.

CHAPTER SEVEN
'I TOOK DRUGS'

Katie and Alex had been married for some months now, but try as they might, they could not separate themselves from Pete. The revelation that she often called Alex 'Pete' by accident made it clear that Katie still harboured some feelings for her ex-husband and now she was prepared to reveal quite how traumatised she had been when Pete finally left. She started off with post-natal depression, which promptly turned into something far worse.

'My depression got so bad that I actually turned to drugs,' Katie revealed. 'I was desperate to get out of my head. After I took it, I thought this feels good. Suddenly I started to feel really strange, my heart seemed to be racing fast. In bed, sleep was out of the question as I lay there wide awake, tormenting myself with thoughts, convinced I was going to die.'

But that was as nothing compared to what happened when Pete eventually walked out. 'Shortly afterwards, I considered killing myself after Peter threatened to leave when I told him I'd taken a drug,' Katie continued. 'Thinking I didn't have Pete any more, I was distraught and desperate: what am I going to do? I've ruined everything. I seriously thought, shall I just end it now, drive into this wall and kill myself? Then I thought, what is wrong with me? You can't do this to the kids, to Pete, to your mum. You're stronger than this. Pull yourself together. Eventually, I had to spend some time at The Priory. I went along to speak to the doctor there, I got everything off my chest.'

She might have been feeling better, but the stories about Pete continued to swirl around – and the name Kerry Katona kept creeping in. Not only had Pete point-blank denied the two were an item, but he was shortly to take legal action against papers who were insinuating that this was indeed the case, and yet the two continued to be linked. The latest story was that Kerry had seen a psychic, which had not only given her a whole new lease of life but was impacting on her romantic side, too.

'Kerry honestly believes her sessions with the psychic

have saved her life,' said a source. 'She was depressed and hated her figure but now she feels reborn after seeing her. The psychic exorcised Kerry's demons and now Kerry keeps saying she owes everything to this woman. Kerry went through a process of psychic healing, which she said felt similar to hypnotherapy. After a course of sessions, Kerry was told to get rid of Mark as he was eating away at her soul and filling her body and mind with negative energy. Kerry also managed to cure her over-eating with help from the spiritual reader. The medium told Kerry to stop worrying about being alone and to focus on her future, which will be full of love and happiness. She told Kerry she will definitely fall in love and remarry. She also said it'll be to someone she already knows and feels a strong bond with, someone already right under her nose.'

Whoever could that be?

Pete was certainly becoming a pretty sought-after figure, as far as women were concerned. Laura White, of *X Factor* fame, had been supporting him on his national tour: they ended up duetting and there was talk of future collaboration. Nor would the Kerry rumours go away. She had been present at a party given by Pete and had bumped into a journalist from the *News of the World*, who told her that her ex-husband Mark was bad news: 'He's not going to like any of this, but I knew what you were saying at the time about what I was doing was true,' she told the journalist. 'I just didn't have the strength to get out of the marriage and stop. But now it's different – I want you to help me find a nice new man!'

Matters then turned nasty, as they were so easily prone to do. There had been constant rows about the children, especially Princess, with Pete getting angry about Katie using hair straighteners on her, or daubing her with make-up: now, however, he was deeply concerned when he saw what he thought were bruises on Princess's face. In actual fact, it was smudged mascara, but before he discovered that, Pete got on to his lawyers, who then called Katie. She, in turn, rang the police.

'It shows how bad relations have got between Katie and Peter that they can't even talk to each other – and are desperately looking for signs the other is a bad parent, even though they both dote on the kids,' said a source close to the duo. 'It's amazing they would rather go to their lawyers and the police over something that could be easily sorted if they just picked up the phone and spoke to each other.'

Pete had obviously overreacted and was even beginning to sound a little defensive. To be concerned about his two-year-old daughter wearing make-up was one thing; to confuse it with bruising quite another.

Indeed, unusually for him, it seemed as if for once he might have been in the wrong, something he clearly wanted to set straight.

'Basically, Princess arrived at my house with some bruises on her face and body a couple of weeks ago and I contacted my lawyers so they could find out from Kate what had happened,' he wrote in his magazine column. 'The story in the paper said that the bruises were, in fact, smudged mascara but this isn't true. I wasn't accusing Kate of anything at all, but as [Princess's] father I just wanted to find out if there was anything I should know. Why the police got involved, I have no idea. There was absolutely no need for them to come round, and when they did, they said everything was fine. I just made a polite inquiry about my daughter that got completely out of hand.'

But there was no reasoning with any of the trio these days. It took just the slightest mishap for the roof to fall in: none of them seemed able to react rationally or, indeed, to calm down. Alex got involved: 'I didn't want to discuss this last week as I thought it was a private matter, but I feel we need to get our side across,' he wrote in his magazine column. 'Princess left our care in perfect, happy health, so we were extremely concerned to be told she had bruises and two black eyes. As anyone in their right mind would do, I immediately contacted the police. Although the kids are not of my blood, I love and adore them and am very protective – and that goes doubly for Kate, who is an excellent mum. After examining Princess, the police sergeant told us there was no bruising on Princess that a two-year-old wouldn't have from simply being a toddler and she definitely didn't have any black eyes. Despite being relaxed, me and Kate were very miffed about the experience.'

Certainly, the insinuations were unpleasant and the fact that the three children were not actually Alex's appeared to make him ever keener to have some of his own. There were fresh reports that the couple were still trying for a baby and had resorted to IVF to speed matters up a bit. 'Katie and Alex really want a child to cement their relationship,' said a friend.

Then there was the wedding to plan for the summer. Given the temperament of everyone involved, there was clearly no way this would ever be a discreet affair, but according to Alex, there were thoughts about making it even more OTT than the previous outing between Katie and Pete. Indeed, he was thinking of a *Star Wars* theme.

'I drove past a *Star Wars* fancy-dress store and thought it would be a really fun theme for the wedding,' he revealed. 'It would be a giggle. Katie and me could go as Princess Leia and Darth Vader – I'm up for that idea. I wouldn't say I'm a *Star Wars* fan –

I'm a *Star Wars* freak! I really love the films. In my mum's loft I've got a Millennium Falcon and loads of other toys. I've even got a Death Star that must be worth about £2,000. At our wedding there will be no fairytale coaches – Katie's done that, let's keep it a bit more sane. Nothing's finalised for the wedding but it's going to be good, it's really exciting.'

It was also, if truth be told, unlikely to be on a *Star Wars* theme.

All of this increased exposure, however, was doing Alex no harm at all. One of the ways in which Katie had made her fortune had been through product endorsements and such was the interest in Alex now that it seemed he might be able to do the same. 'I might do an aftershave range for Christmas. Splash on a dab of the Reidinator, I say!' he announced cheerily. 'I had meetings about a few possible deals last week that I am really excited about, including one for my own fight clothing brand and sport supplements. I am also talking about two new TV shows.'

Again, just as with Pete, Katie and Alex together were proving to be dynamite. Whatever the naysayers might observe on the state of the marriage, it was clear that the two of them were convinced there was every reason to make a go of it. They had too much to lose should they part.

But the baby issue refused to go away. Alex himself

had once fuelled speculation that his new wife was with child when he answered a question as to whether she was pregnant with the words, 'Maybe, maybe not.' Now, however, he felt it was all becoming a little too intrusive and he wanted to put a stop to it: 'I can tell you she's not pregnant at the moment,' he stated.

Of course, the other issue that wouldn't go away was Pete. After the kiss-and-tell fiasco in the wake of his fling with Maddy Ford, he was clearly feeling more cautious about leaving hostages to fortune as far as his private life was concerned and so he came clean about the fact that he had started seeing other women again. But there was one woman he definitely wasn't seeing. 'For those of you who are interested, I can confirm that I am still single, but that I am very much back on the dating scene,' he declared. 'But I won't be telling you anything until I've met someone I'm serious about. False stories are written about me all the time, the latest one being that I'm romantically linked to my old pal Kerry Katona.'

And there was, according to everyone involved, no chance of his going there.

Even though Alex had denied it, rumours continued to circulate about whether Katie was or wasn't pregnant and fuel was added to the fire when she announced that she would not be running the 2010 marathon. So, what was the real reason behind that?

'It is with great regret that I'm going to have to pull out of this year's Virgin London Marathon,' she said. 'Training has been going really well, and I was really looking forward to running again this year to raise as much money as possible for Vision, but I have been advised by doctors I should not compete this year. I wish everyone the best of luck. I know how hard this is, so I have nothing but admiration for each and every runner. Hope to see you in 2011.'

Could she be having a baby after all?

In the meantime, the feud with Kerry rumbled on. Katie was adamant that she couldn't have cared less about the growing friendship between her husband and her one-time friend, but behind the scenes observers were not so sure. What made matters worse was that Kerry was blossoming. Gone was the overweight drug addict of a few years previously, in its place a slim, lithe and fresh-faced girl: the Kerry of yesteryear. And the transformation was solely down to Claire Powell: in taking Kerry so firmly in hand, she had proved, for all the world to see, quite what an amazing effect she could have on the clients who let her take control.

Katie, of course, had done nothing of the sort. Almost congenitally unable to let anyone else guide her, she was no fan of what she saw to be Claire's controlling side. But now, from the outside, it was almost beginning to look as if it were she and Alex up against the gang of three. Kerry was blooming, Pete had cheered up, while Claire looked after their careers with a masterly ease – and the growing friendship between Pete and Kerry seemed to be rubbing salt into the wound.

There was also the fact that the break-up of the two marriages had been very different. Pete and Katie had been at the top of their particular type of celebrity tree: King and Queen of all they surveyed in the world of reality TV, effortlessly dominating the magazines that followed their every action with breathless enthusiasm, head and shoulders above the rest. They had accumulated enormous wealth – Katie alone was worth at least £30 million – and although they were known to bicker, as witnessed on their reality television show, they still seemed a pretty devoted and committed couple. Or so it had appeared.

Kerry's marriage, on the other hand, had been a car crash right from the beginning. Thrown into terrible depths of depression and despair when her first husband, Brian McFadden, walked out, Kerry had been too vulnerable and frail to see what a disaster it would be to tie her fortunes to a man like Mark Croft. Sure enough, she had learned the error of her ways when he was branded a cheat and who knows what else. As they frittered theit way through Kerry's multi-million fortune, eventually ending up with her going bankrupt, she fell ever lower down the scale.

Watching from the outside, friends were in despair: Croft was seemingly bad news, yet no one seemed able to bring Kerry to her senses – even when she was pictured snorting cocaine and even though she herself said that she thought Mark was behind the pictures. The former Atomic Kitten star looked to be headed into that grey world of the celebrity who had had it all and threw it all away: there seemed no depths to which she might not sink.

But look what happened then. Katie's seemingly perfect marriage fell apart and shortly afterwards, so did she, going out partying, allowing her name to be linked with a series of men and very publicly showing herself to be unable to take the strain. And after years of being the dominant one in the marriage, it was Pete who walked out – sweet, sensitive, put-upon Pete, who was now being talked about as a near saint for having suffered her for all those years. The humiliation would have been hideous, whatever else was going on in the outer world, but just as Katie was beginning to fall apart, Kerry, her erstwhile friend and now deadly rival, was finally beginning to get it together again.

It was Kerry who booted Mark out of the house and the marriage, not the other way around. It was Kerry who, after years of being the put upon spouse, finally found the strength to walk away from it, while Mark was left out in the cold. In short, it was Kerry who had done exactly what Pete had done (although no one could ever compare Katie to Mark Croft) and walked away from a marriage that was no longer making her happy. Was it any wonder the two were getting on so well?

Katie could not have been pleased about it: out of all the people in the world for Pete to become friendly with, this was without a doubt the scenario that would have pleased her least. She must have realised, too, that Kerry and Pete would not have been human not to enjoy the situation, at least a little bit. Revenge, if either of them thought about it in that way, must have tasted pretty sweet.

Katie could be forgiven for not feeling very happy and so she responded in the way she knew best – by upping the stakes. Australia had come to have a particular resonance in this story, not least because it was where Pete was brought up, where the two had met in the celebrity jungle – which Katie had so recently revisited – and to which she had recently forbidden Pete to take the kids on holiday, which she was legally entitled to do. So what better than to bring

Australia into it, while she was feeling more than a little on edge?

Whether or not she fully intended to go ahead with it was not clear, but Katie let it be known that she was planning a long summer break out there, in Pete's old hunting grounds. 'Katie is still annoyed by Pete supposedly dating her former friend Kerry Katona,' said a source. 'She thinks that by being seen out loads in Australia – where much of his family is based – it will get to him. She's hoping to rent a gorgeous house in the late summer.' In actual fact, given the proximity to Pete's family, it would almost certainly have ended up making everything a whole lot worse.

Then there was the fact that whatever Katie might say about moving on, there were still very strong suspicions in many people's minds that she hadn't even begun to get over Pete. After her initial and very public devastation when he first walked out, there had been reports of her leaving texts for her ex, begging him for another chance and trying to make up for what had gone wrong. There had even been stories that she had left a recording of herself singing, 'I Will Always Love You' on his phone – certainly, it seemed she was not as indifferent as she so often claimed. The fact that Pete would still not speak to her face-to-face continued to rile her, too: she had lost control of the situation and Katie couldn't bear that. And so rumours of private contretemps continued to surface – the situation was a long way from calming down.

It had been known that Katie continued to phone Pete on a very regular basis, calls that it was said he tried to avoid, but according to some people, Alex hadn't realised the full scale of what was going on. It was brought home to him very sharply, however, when he saw Katie's phone bill, which rather made the point about how much she'd been calling her ex.

'Alex thought Jordan called Pete from time to time about the kids,' revealed a source. 'But he wasn't prepared for what he saw on the phone bill. His heart sank. Call after call was to Pete ... It was devastating for him. She asks the kids to put daddy on the phone. Pete agrees to talk to Jordan if it's about Princess or Junior, but he knows she's only doing it so she can speak to him.'

It was getting to a state where Pete was said to be considering changing the number on his phone – not that it would really make a difference. The two of them had two children together, and divorce or no divorce, were bound by the ties of parenthood. Whatever Pete's phone number, the situation was not about to change.

Even so, it was tempting to change the number. 'It's got that bad,' continued the source. 'He doesn't want to be pestered. Alex had been ignoring the signs. Even when she stood outside Pete's house, screaming for him to come out, Alex still persuaded himself that she didn't have a problem. Jordan's always got the excuse that she needs to talk to Pete about the kids. Alex understands that but he thinks she should still erase the number from her mobile ... He's not happy.'

But this was the world in which he was now living. Katie and Pete's life was so different from the vast majority of people's that they might be forgiven for not realising just how unusual their existence had become. Even other reality TV stars, including Kerry Katona, did not lead their life in front of the cameras 24/7 in the way that Katie and Pete did, and as a result, everything had become far more intense than it would have done under normal circumstances, with emotions magnified and heightened. It was hardly surprising, because for years now they had been called upon to provide drama for the camera, but the downside was that both seemed to have a problem with keeping it all under control.

And now that Alex was part of that world, he was increasingly affected by it all. On the one hand, he was becoming aware of quite what he had let himself in for: the constant cameras and attention, the drama, the crises that would spring out of nowhere, and on the other, he was increasingly affected by it himself. Don't make a drama out of a crisis? For Katie and

Pete, it had been the modus operandi for years now and if nothing else, that hadn't changed. Both knew that it was vital to maintain the public's interest if they wanted to stay at the (very lucrative) centre of attention. And so it went on.

There was also the not-so-minor matter of Alex's training, which was also affected by the demands of his new life. Before he met Katie, Alex trained twice a day, five out of six days a week, but now there was no time at all. In an interview that Alex gave in 2006, years before he gravitated into the irresistible environment surrounding Katie Price, he drew a very revealing picture of what life was like then – and of course, it had changed beyond compare.

There was, in this early account of Alex's life, no mention of cross-dressing, reality television or any of the other areas that he had so recently made his own. 'If I'm feeling tired, I try to take a day off,' he said. 'I always try to take one day a week off, but sometimes it doesn't happen. But if I'm having a busy schedule, the life of a fighter isn't set in concrete, schedule-wise. Fighting isn't the most lucrative sport, so I have to pick up pieces here and there, and that of course affects my training program. If something comes in, I think: what should I do – go down the gym or put food on the table?'

At this stage, Alex continued to work as a bouncer

to help make ends meet. His acting career seemed to be behind him and so he was concentrating hard on making a go of fighting. There was no sign that his life was to veer off in a dramatically different direction – but equally, reading the comments he made back then, came a very strong indication that if he were to start spending time with someone like Katie, he simply wouldn't be able to keep up the strict regime he'd set for himself.

'I don't go mad all the time,' he continued. 'But sometimes it gets a bit more intense. Yesterday, I trained four times. But I'm feeling it today. I want to have a good break for the rest of the day, although I'm sparring later this evening, so I'll just take it easy until tonight and then I'll step it up.'

Everything centred on his fighting back then. He had to train constantly and on top of that, maintain the right weight. 'Normally, I need to cut weight,' he explained. 'I'm quite heavy at the moment, so I need to do a lot of running and training. I fight as a Middleweight, but presently I'm heavier than a Light-Heavy, which is crazy. When I lose that poundage I'll be so powerful. I feel powerful at the moment. And what I do – the Americans, especially, are great at it – I cut weight, because we weigh-in the day before.'

How to combine a training schedule like that with life as Katie's consort would prove a challenge to anyone and indeed, it was beginning to show. Alex looked as rugged and fit as ever, but there were increasing fears from those close to him that he just wasn't putting in the hours he needed as a fighter. But then, there was the chance of an acting career. Meanwhile, Roxanne, his cross-dressing alter ego, had taken a bow and left the stage. Alex was adamant that side of his life didn't exist anymore.

Katie, Pete and Alex – and now, perhaps, Kerry Katona, too – the whole circus was getting completely out of control. And yet the story continued to fascinate as never before. Nor did recent events appear to have harmed anyone, as far as popularity was concerned: although Pete and Kerry were blossoming under the guidance of Claire Powell, Katie and Alex were doing pretty well for themselves, too. Every week the magazines featured the four of them in some shape or form on the cover. Newspapers continued to speculate about the exact nature of the relationships of everyone involved. Their stories, their lives, were now so much in the public domain that the nation felt they knew them personally. All were going from strength to strength.

And Alex, perhaps the least media-savvy of all, was prospering, too. His appearance belied the reality: before his marriage to Katie, he was actually just a nice boy, albeit a slightly exhibitionist one, who was still living with his mum and dad. Now he was becoming a household name, with all the opportunities that went with it, all the possibilities for the future, all to play for ahead.

Alex was also the least tormented of them all: he was the only one in the quartet not to have suffered a very public and traumatic divorce. A sweetness was evident in his nature, and his level-headedness provided the grounding that Katie needed.

Pete, meanwhile, for all that he found it sometimes difficult to deal with, was well aware that life had given him a second chance. These days, he was noticeably more relaxed, too. He had lost a great deal of weight after the initial separation, but the strain he'd been under seemed to be leaving him. He was looking happier than he had done for years in his own skin. And the kiss-and-tell might have been embarrassing, but at least it got everything out in the open. Indeed, for the first time since the divorce, Pete was beginning to think he might be ready to date again.

And so they were all coming through in their own way, all gaining something from the chaos surrounding them, a new order in their lives was beginning to emerge. There was just one thing lacking: Katie might still harbour ambiguous feelings towards Pete, but Alex was her husband now and she wanted to build up a life with him. She was still young, they both were, and still looked forward to a future together and all that awaited them. There were deals to be done and in Alex's case, perhaps an acting career to be resumed. Then there was the challenge of cracking the States, something Katie had never quite managed with Pete, but was looking forward to trying to do so again with Alex.

Despite all this, one element was still missing: Katie still wanted to be 'Reidinated'. She and Alex wanted to cement their relationship with a child of their own.

CHAPTER EIGHT
A HONEYMOON
IN EGYPT

It was an unusual way to start a honeymoon, but then there was nothing usual about the lifestyle lived by Katie Price. The wedding had been some months back, of course, but the newlyweds had been so busy then that they hadn't had time to celebrate. Now, at last, they were making time to celebrate their wedding (well, the *first* of their weddings – the second was still some months away) with a break in the Egyptian resort of Sharm el-Sheikh.

The resort was a luxury one, exactly the sort of place where a young couple in love would want to spend their time getting to know one another. But eyebrows were raised from the start because they were not alone: the two had Harvey with them – perhaps understandable, as Pete was off in Dubai with Junior and Princess – but what was slightly more surprising was that friends had accompanied them, too. And not just any old friends: these friends were Andrew Gould, Katie's riding instructor, whose friendship with Katie had caused Pete to erupt in jealousy and fury just about a year previously, Andrew's wife Polly and the Goulds' two children.

Nor was it just the presence of another family on the honeymoon that took observers aback, but the timing of it, too. Alex's fight with Tom 'Kong' Watson was less than a month away and it was expected that he would be training hard, not travelling to five-star resorts to eat, drink and be merry. Watson himself was very unimpressed, labelling Alex, '...a complete joke. I fully expect him to pull out of this fight,' and went on, 'but I will keep training as if he isn't.'

With her usual unerring ability to make a drama out of every aspect of her life, however, Katie managed to time the honeymoon, totally unwittingly, with a terror alert. The resort was a focus for Western tourists: the Israeli government issued a warning to its citizens about a potential terrorist attack. It goes without saying that Katie could not possibly have known this was going to happen – indeed, it's highly unlikely she'd have visited the resort if she did – but it was yet another example of the fact that she couldn't do anything in her life without attracting attention. It was a unique talent to have, and one that she was able to exploit to the full.

As if potential terrorist attacks, Alex's lack of training and the presence on the honeymoon with her second husband of the man, who might have played a part in the divorce from the first were not enough, increasingly bizarre stories began to surface about what Katie was, and wasn't able to get up to while she was out there in the sun. Diving was apparently a no-no because of what it might do to her breast implants. 'There have been scare stories about implants exploding underwater,' said a source. 'Research has shown this is unlikely but they do fill with air bubbles as the pressure increases and can change size underwater. Implants also affect buoyancy so she'd have to make extra efforts to stay afloat. Given the risks, and how long she has spent perfecting her boobs, it is unlikely Kate will go ahead.'

Something else that didn't go ahead was Alex's fight. Just as Tom Watson and a fair few others had predicted, Alex pulled out; it was almost certainly a wise decision because whatever he might have been doing previously, he wasn't training hard enough now. He risked a real injury if he went ahead, and if truth be told, these days it was looking as if he had bigger fish to fry. 'Alex Reid has sustained an injury during the filming of his Bravo *Fight Of His Life* programme,' said his spokesman. 'He has seen numerous doctors and specialists, all advising him to not train at the level required in the lead-up to a fight. In light of this, Alex will unfortunately be postponing his fight on May 15 with Tom "Kong" Watson. Alex will be seeing a BAMMA doctor upon his return to further assess the injury and work towards a new date. Alex is gutted to postpone the fight and is looking forward to taking on his competitor.'

At least the luxury of his surroundings might help him to cope with the pain.

There were, however, quite a few considerations regarding the future, not least the fact that Alex really had a chance to make something of himself if he played his cards right. Fighting was one option but so, too, was acting. 'I might have another ten years [left in fighting] but there are lots of other exciting things on the horizon,' he told one interviewer. 'In fact, I'm going for an audition for a BBC drama, the biggest-budgeted thing they've ever done. I want to leave my mark on society, for people to think, "Yeah, he was something."'

Back in the UK, Katie's name came up in a different and totally unexpected context when it was suggested that she might one day replace Simon Cowell on *Britain's Got Talent*. The man himself was thinking that the day when he'd be stepping down himself was looming and who better to replace him than a woman who was one of the world's best at garnering publicity?

'I am looking at whether I have a different role next year,' Cowell revealed in an interview. 'I am considering coming just for the semi-finals. I like the show, but it takes a hell of a lot of time. You sit there watching horrific acts and you think, I genuinely can't do this any more. Can I see it working without me? Yes.' As for Katie – 'Well, those are your words, not mine. But Jordan is a friend. It's too early to say what will happen. Whoever takes over has to really know what they are talking about. You have to spot a star, nurture them, mentor them.'

Whether Katie really could be suitable for that type of role was a moot point but the very fact that she was mentioned in conjunction with it showed that the rest of the entertainment industry recognised her as a complete pro.

Not to be outdone, Pete opened up about the fact that he'd also been offered a big judging role in reality TV, this one being the Australian version of *The X Factor*. Because of the distances involved, he'd eventually declined, though. 'I hate turning down fantastic opportunities like this and I would have loved to have taken part, but my children absolutely come first and there is no way I could be apart from them for that long. It would kill me,' he wrote.

Even this provoked controversy, with Simon Cowell's production company, SyCo, denying that Pete had ever been approached. 'Peter Andre has never been offered any role on *The X Factor* in any country,' said a spokesman.

A clearly angry Claire Powell, Pete's manager, begged to differ: 'We had an email into our office about three weeks ago,' she said. 'It came from Fremantle, who co-produce *The X Factor*, asking whether Peter would be involved in Australia's edition. We had a serious discussion about it. Why on earth would Peter or any of us make that up?' Why indeed?

Besides, life was treating him pretty well. Pete had just splashed out £2 million on a new house in West Sussex, which was just what he had been looking for: 'He's been on the hunt for a new place for months and now he has taken the plunge,' revealed a source, pointing out that Tom Cruise owned a property nearby. 'It is a brand-new house with seven bedrooms, so there is plenty of space for the kids and the rest of his family. It has beautiful views and every luxury inside. This is a place where Pete can settle down and be really happy. It is a peaceful spot and gives lots of privacy – just the place to start afresh.' And that was certainly what he appeared to be doing now.

Pete and Kerry-related rumours were still going strong, however, and Katie was forced once again to deny that she gave them a second thought. After all, it was she who had married again, not Pete, and now she was on her honeymoon. 'The whole Peter/Kerry thing really does not worry me whatsoever,' she wrote on her blog. 'I have moved on like you would not believe, I think you all know that now, and the papers can carry on writing what they want, and the magazines.' It was fortunate that she took that attitude because that was exactly what the press continued to do, with no one really able to work out what the truth was. And did Katie care? Apparently not, it seemed.

But if reports coming out of Egypt were to be believed, the honeymoon was not going according to plan. Katie and Alex were said to be rowing constantly and far from celebrating their marriage, both doubted whether they'd done the right thing. Indeed, Katie was heard to yell, 'I made a big mistake marrying you!' Hardly love's young dream.

'It was supposed to be the time for love and romance,' said a source. 'But they're at each other's throats. It won't last till Christmas at this rate. Everybody's talking about the Iceland volcano but that's not the only thing that's blowing up abroad. Alex is on the verge of coming home – if he can get a flight!' (In fact, the Icelandic volcano didn't just affect Katie and Alex – it also left Pete and the two children stranded in Dubai.) While he wouldn't have dreamt of commenting on the reports, clearly Pete himself felt it was a mistake to rush into a new relationship so quickly. 'A survey revealed last week that it takes the average person at least 18 months to recover from a divorce,' he wrote in his magazine column. 'I would totally agree with this. If you really loved them, you don't get over it just like that. These things take time.' He didn't say any more, but then he didn't need to – no one would have been in much doubt as to what he meant.

Alex must have got the message too, although he certainly didn't say as much. Indeed, it looked as if he was becoming fully aware of the danger of getting drawn into a very public tiff with his predecessor – especially if the rumours about trouble in paradise were true – and was beginning to show signs of distancing himself from it all. 'People always ask me about Pete, but I'm not saying anything more on him,' he announced rather belatedly. 'I am not interested – he is not on my mind. How long are people going to ask me about him for? I am just getting on with my own life.'

This had the faintest reek of Katie's repeated protestations that she was over her former husband and had moved on, but no matter. Alex was wising up to the downside of very public spats.

Incredibly, given the amount of trouble it had caused last time around, Katie was doing exactly what she'd done with Pete and had become extremely competitive with her new husband about their respective reality TV shows. She constantly compared the ratings, gloating over the fact that she was doing better than Alex, even taunting him at times. 'Katie wouldn't let it go,' said a source. 'She told Alex, "Don't give up the day job." He was gutted.'

Would she never learn? That urge to humiliate the man in her life always seemed to resurface, even when things were going well. And despite the more controversial elements of his lifestyle, Alex, like Pete, was a fundamentally nice guy. But Katie was so headstrong and volatile that she simply didn't seem to see that she was risking another disaster: this was the time to be consolidating their relationship, not harming it from within.

The desire to upstage her men folk might endlessly speculated upon and related back to other aspects of her life: the photographer who wasn't what he seemed and the unfaithful exes, but it was also indicative of a profoundly self-destructive streak, too. Underneath all the glitz and the glamour, it was sometimes possible to view a very different Katie – one who had suffered post-natal depression, who had once attempted suicide in the wake of her split from Dane Bowers, even though she later said it hadn't been a very serious attempt; a woman who had turned to drugs when her husband walked out. That Katie was altogether a more fragile creature than the one now bellowing belligerently at her new husband. Sometimes it almost seemed as if she was trying to destroy herself from within: she obviously didn't realise what she was doing and as she dominated everyone around her, there was nothing or no one to stop her. It was a vicious circle with no easy way out.

Still, she was clearly an inspiration to a certain type of man. Back in Blighty, *Britain's Got Talent* had returned to the television screens, with one contestant – a 22-year-old male model called Adam Miller – citing Katie as a particular inspiration. Indeed, it turned out they'd already met. Adam appeared on the show as a female impersonator, dancing and lip-synching to 'Circus' by Britney Spears while dressed in a ringmaster's outfit, just like Britney herself. Judges Piers Morgan, Amanda Holden and Louis Walsh (standing in for a sickly Simon Cowell) were impressed and gave him a treble 'yes'. But it was Katie he really looked up to, as he made clear in an interview after the show.

'Amanda Holden said I gave a perfect, polished performance,' he said. 'Piers Morgan said it was like watching Britney herself and that I was the best female impersonator he'd seen. I'm trying to become the male Katie Price and turn myself into the most perfect male model.'

This was to be accomplished via £52,000-worth of plastic surgery – and a meeting with Andrew Gould.

'I emailed him to say I wanted to go riding,' Adam continued. 'We made friends and then last June, nights later, we went out with Katie and she bought me drinks all night. She told me I was gorgeous the way I was, but advised me on getting my teeth done. I told her she was my idol and I wanted to be as successful as her. She was really flattered.'

As for the surgery, to be paid for by his mum and his partner – 'I'm just getting my inheritance early. My mum thinks I shouldn't mess with my body but I'm nearly 23, so she has to stand by me. I've been called spoilt before as I've done things like order a Rolls-Royce to school when I was younger and got my mum to splash out so I can live the celebrity lifestyle but I don't think I'm any more spoilt than other people.'

He was certainly the kind of man Katie adored.

But back in the world of her ex and present

husbands, Katie certainly showed that she knew how to hurt. She now revealed that the children had started to call Alex 'Daddy', with all the implications that involved: Pete was clearly the target here. 'Harvey likes to know there's a man about the house,' said Katie. 'They all actually call him "Daddy Alex" now. And they call his [Alex's] parents "Grandma Carol" and "Grandpa Bob". Alex is Daddy Alex, and it's all good because when me and Alex have one it will be less confusing for them – they don't just call him Daddy, he's Daddy Alex. Junior loves it because he's got a punch bag. Alex changed Princess's nappy for the first time the other day and it was a number two! It was funny. The kids get on with him really well and I'm pleased about that. I wouldn't have married Alex otherwise. They have someone they can look up to in Alex.'

Nonetheless, the presence of Pete loomed large. He had been held up in Dubai because of the volcanic dust cloud causing havoc to global flight schedules and had been pictured topless and deeply tanned, looking better than he had in years. Like Katie, he had lost a great deal of weight after the split and sources were not slow to point out the differences between his physique and Alex's, which, what with less training and more eating, was a little more robust than it had once been. Katie was not pleased and started threatening to put him on a diet. She certainly wasn't going to let Pete get one up there.

'In their business, image is everything,' said a friend. 'Kate is worried if he lets himself go there will be consequences for their money-earning potential. The new pictures of Pete will bring home to her how much she wants her man to stay looking good. She wants him put on a strict eating plan. She knows that if he loses his physique, Alex will find it hard to fight.'

Not that he was alone in having put on a bit of weight. Like Pete, Katie and Alex had found themselves marooned for dust cloud-related reasons and had had to extend their stay at the Egyptian resort. This had the result that Katie was exposed to an awful lot of delicious and tempting food – and was giving in to it, too.

'On the beach, she was showing a bit of spare tyre – unheard of for Katie,' one onlooker remarked. 'It's another blow for her – she prides herself on being super-skinny.'

So, it wasn't only Alex who was being put on rations – Katie had to be careful, too.

It must have been all the more galling then that Kerry Katona continued to bloom. Her healthy new lifestyle was already showing amazing results: Kerry looked more svelte than she had in years. She was garnering a lot of public sympathy as well, for she, too, was in the midst of a dreadful and public row with her first husband: she had given an interview in which she said that Brian (now Brian, not Bryan) rarely saw his children and that the younger, Lily, didn't really know who he was.

Brian did not take this well and took to Twitter. 'FACT... I call my girls at least twice a week and have a beautiful relationship with my daughters,' he tweeted. 'I've kept my silence too long and I can't keep it any more. It's killing me and my beautiful fiancée and my mum and dad and friends. ENOUGH. Kerry Katona, you are dead to me!' He then went on to call her a 'pig-faced mole.'

If this was meant to re-establish him as the good guy, however, it didn't work. There was widespread sympathy for Kerry, especially now that she'd got rid of Mark, and given that it was Brian who had dumped Kerry when the children were still very young, his remarks did not go down well. Indeed, shortly after posting them, he took them down.

'He took the comments down because he doesn't want to stoop to Kerry's level,' said a friend. 'It's unlikely they'll ever speak again.'

But their little girl Molly's first communion was coming up, an event for which Brian would return to the UK, and there were real fears that it could be ruined by the row that had broken out between her parents. None of the parties involved seemed to be backing down, either. 'Brian knows this is a big deal for his little girls and promised he would do his utmost to come back to be there for them,' said a source. 'This was being planned way before Kerry started kicking off. His tirades on Twitter are just an indication of what is said privately about her. He wants to confront her about what she's doing and demand she stop involving him. Brian has promised his mum that he will do his best not to flare up in front of the kids. But having the Katona and McFadden families in the same room could cause all kinds of bust-ups. Kerry's mum Sue has not seen Brian since he slated her for being a bad mother. And Kerry isn't shy. But she has been trying to turn a corner, so this may give them a chance to put everything behind them.'

Fat chance! The bitterness between Kerry and Brian was so great that there was little hope of a truce any time soon. But it must have been mystifying to Katie as to why the public had taken Kerry's side when she divorced Brian, but not Katie's when she divorced Pete. After all, both had their husbands walk out on them and while Katie might have turned to the odd narcotic for comfort, it was nothing like Kerry's drug binges with Mark that had gone on for days. Nor had she been financially irresponsible like

Kerry, who had been made bankrupt, or taken up with a man like Mark Croft. And yet the public was palpably willing Kerry back to health and a good state of wellbeing, while Katie was still getting it in the neck from all sides.

One reason for this, although she probably didn't realise it, was that unlike Kerry, Katie demanded to be in control at all times. Unlike Kerry, she had an extremely domineering personality and always put herself first, while Kerry went rather too far in the opposite direction. Although Katie had undeniably loved Pete and then Alex, there was no question of either ever being allowed to overshadow her.

Still, public opinion must have been very perplexing for Katie and neither was the couple attracting any sympathy about their so-far unsuccessful attempts to have a baby. The two were photographed outside a fertility clinic in London, having finally got back from their extended honeymoon: clearly, it was finally too much for Alex, who lunged out at the photographers. Given the pressure he must have been under, the only wonder was that it hadn't happened before.

'Alex seemed to have lost it,' said one onlooker. 'He is normally a calm guy but in recent weeks, it just seems like things have got to him. He doesn't look like he is dealing with fame at all. He felt the paparazzi were being very intrusive and were blocking his path,' said his spokesperson. 'Therefore he called the police.'

It was the first sign that the duo really were beginning to feel the strain. For months now, they had courted not only publicity, but controversy, too and if their aim was to become the prime topic of conversation on everyone's lips, then they had certainly succeeded. But the pressure was relentless and even Katie sometimes looked as if she was feeling the strain.

Alex had hinted as much in the past. 'I'm not in love with being noticed all the time,' he'd said in an interview just before they went on honeymoon. 'All of a sudden, everyone seems to know 90 per cent of everything about me. I've got to be a bit more careful about what I say, but I'm still trying to be true to myself. Katie nearly got run over by a paparazzi [sic] yesterday. I got so angry, I wanted to kill him. I don't get to spend as much time with my new family as I'd like. It's hard, sometimes, to get the balance right. But I love the kids – Princess gives me endless cuddles and Junior has perfected a lot of kickboxing moves and loves beating me up.'

Some consolation perhaps, but Alex was obviously finding it harder to cope than he'd expected.

Nor were matters helped when property guru Kirstie Allsopp publicly criticised the whole set-up, in particular the way the children had been put in the public eye. 'As far as Katie Price is concerned, she might as well just put her children up a chimney to earn some money. Everyone knows who they are. They have no chance in later life of leading private lives,' declared Kirstie. 'You really shouldn't criticise people in the public eye, but I think someone does have to say: "Think twice before you have your children photographed". It's one thing to turn up to a première or a party, it's another to put them through a photo shoot. By making them famous, you are removing their right to make that decision themselves.'

She herself would herself love to develop a range of children's clothes, Kirstie continued, but she, 'just couldn't use my children as models.'

Katie was not slow to respond. 'Who's Kirstie Allsopp?' she demanded to know. 'I have never even heard of her, so it's bizarre and quite funny that she is just using my name to further her own career.'

A source stepped in: 'Kirstie just seems yet another person who is badmouthing Katie to get publicity for themselves,' he said. 'It just seems unfair she has picked up on Katie when Peter is on the cover of magazines with the kids.'

Behind the scenes Katie was smarting, as that reference to Pete made clear. Both appeared regularly with their children in public and both featured them on their reality TV shows, so why was Katie the one being singled out for criticism?

Indeed, Pete was coming across brilliantly, as always. He, too, had finally managed to make it back from Dubai and explained the concerns that parents with their children in tow have to be aware of: 'As a parent you can't rule anything out and it is a very scary thought,' he said. '[But] Junior has so many friends – everyone is looking out for him. I had ten kids come up to me and told me that Junior was talking to a girl.'

It was so unfair, but Katie simply didn't manage to come across like that. And those rumours about the true state of her marriage refused to go away. There was more talk of rows behind the scenes while, ominously, Katie didn't appear to think that Alex was her match. Others were concerned that it seemed that Alex was not so much the great love of her life as a break-up fling that had far too quickly turned serious.

More than once in the past it had happened that one of Katie's men avowed that she didn't actually like sex very much and certainly, during her relationship with Pete, it was off the menu for months at a time. But Katie and Alex were still at the stage when they should have been in the first flush of love –

if they were already behaving more like friends than lovers, what might the future possibly hold?

At this point, the focus moved back to Pete. Earlier that year, there had been a huge row when he had almost been reduced to tears live on air on the Sky News programme, *Afternoon Live*, after Kay Burley asked him how he would feel if Alex wanted to adopt his children. On the same programme was a filmed interview with Dwight Yorke, Harvey's father, in which he criticised Pete for having previously said that he wanted to adopt Harvey. The timing of the show was considered sensitive, coming as it did in the immediate aftermath of Katie and Alex's wedding. Pete had actually been booked to talk about his forthcoming album and the public reaction was one of fury, with 881 complaints made to the broadcasting regulator Ofcom. Kay Burley was widely felt to have overstepped the mark and publicly accused of bullying.

In the event she was cleared, with the interview labelled 'persistent and probing' rather than 'bullying and intimidating.' It was, said Ofcom, 'in keeping' with the programme's editorial values to ask about the wedding, given that it was such a major news story: 'Further, it was understandable that the presenter focused on the human interest angle of the wedding by asking Peter Andre for his reaction and how it would impact on their children,' the regulator went on. 'In Ofcom's view, the audience could therefore reasonably have expected the presenter to ask him about the wedding, and the implications of it, given that the interview was taking place on a rolling news programme on the same day that the wedding featured as a major news item. [Pete] knew that the wedding had taken place, was a major news story, and that he would be asked questions about it when he agreed to proceed with the interview.'

As for Kay Burley, 'She also expressed concern about his wellbeing and apologised for any upset the broadcast may have generated. Ofcom also notes that although he appeared upset to some extent by the style of interviewing, Peter Andre is a well-known professional singer with considerable experience of the media, who had agreed to appear on the programme to promote his album, knowing that the wedding of his former wife was a topical news story. Overall, therefore, we concluded that the style of interview did not breach generally accepted standards.'

Pete himself had talked 'candidly and frequently in public' about Katie and the children: 'Therefore the subject of his family and his marriage breakdown has been previously brought to public attention on several occasions and it would not, in Ofcom's opinion, have exceeded viewer expectations for questions on these subjects to be put to him in the context of a programme with a populist news agenda. Kay Burley's approach was persistent and probing, but in Ofcom's view it could not reasonably be described as bullying and intimidating.' And so both programme and presenter were cleared, although the whole subject left a nasty taste in some mouths.

Not that Pete himself had complained. To be fair, he knew what he had put himself up for – Pete had been in show business for a long time now and had learned to take the rough with the smooth. In this, he was very different from Alex, who was still learning how to cope: Pete, although allowing himself to appear very upset, had not lashed out at photographers nor appeared to be out of control at any time since the split. And given the strain that he, too, must have been under, it couldn't have been easy. But this was an episode best judged by all to be left in the past.

Katie herself had objected to Kay's treatment of Pete, but clearly felt it was now time to move on. Besides, there was work to be getting on with. Katie appeared on a new quiz show, *Scream If You Know The Answer*, hosted by Duncan James.

Kerry Katona said nothing either; instead she suggested a holiday with one Peter Andre. The pair had established an increasingly close friendship, both

Above: Dedicated follower of fashion – Peter at the Ed Hardy store launch at London's Westfield shopping centre.

Below: In action during his *Revelation* tour in March 2010.

© *Geoffrey Swaine/Rex Features*

Peter's family have been a great support to him throughout his life.
Above left: With sister Debbie and one of his brothers at the opening
of Debbie's beauty salon in Surfer's Paradise, Australia.

© Icon Images/Rex Feature

Above right: With his brother Michael at a CD signing in Coventry.

© David Hartley/Rex Feature

Below: Enjoying the company of his brothers Mike (*left*) and Danny
(*right*) in Cairns.

© Brian Cassey/Rex Feature

Above: Peter hard at work promoting his cd, *Unconditional – Love Songs*.

© *Geoffrey Swaine/Rex Features*

Below left: A plaster covers up the 'Katie' tattoo on his wedding ring finger.

© *David Hartley/Rex Features*

Below right: Was Peter's t-shirt a message to Alex Reid? The singer had wished his ex-wife well following the news that she was to wed the cage fighter in Las Vegas.

© *Geoffrey Robinson/Rex Features.*

At the launch of his fragrance, Unconditional. © *Mark Campbell/Rex Features*

friend to the fans.

Above: Two admirers steal a kiss from their idol.

© *Geoffrey Robinson/Rex Features*

Below left: Still a crowd-puller – hundreds turned up to this album signing n Cambridge.

© *Geoffrey Robinson/ Rex Features*

Below right: One fan, known as 'The Phantom Hugger' gets to grips with eter outside London Television studios.

© *Beretta/Sims/Rex Features*

Above: Reunited with Ant and Dec for a festive appearance on their *Saturday Night Takeaway* and, *below left,* with Emma Bunton on the same show.

© *ITV/Rex Featur*

Below right: Combining work with his passion for coffee, Peter fronts the new Costa flat white range.

© *Jonathan Hordle/Rex Featur*

Above and below left: Peter often states that his children are his world. Here he is, taking son Junior and daughter Princess to meet Bob the Builder, accompanied by his mother, Thea.

© *Rex Features*

Below right: With Rachel Hunter at the World Music Awards in Monte Carlo.

© *Sipa Press/Rex Features*

Above left: Kerry Katona at a Peter Andre concert. Kerry now shares Peter's management company (*pictured with her above right*) and has moved into a large barn conversion in Surrey so that she can be closer to them (*below*). Kerry and Peter have become close friends since her relocation, but any rumours of a romance have been flatly denied by both parties.

© *Mike Campbell/Rex Features; Beretta/Sims/Rex Features; Rex Features* had young children and both knew everything there was to know about life in the public eye, so why not?

'Peter's been a rock for Kerry the last month or so,' said a friend. 'Kerry will call him at night and they've been texting, too. Pete knows how hard dragging yourself up from the bottom can be, and he's a huge support. She is hoping Pete will consider going away with her and bringing his kids, Junior and Princess. He's been away with model Nicola McLean before as friends and Kerry doesn't see it as anything more than that.'

That was almost certainly true, but no one even bothered to pretend that Katie would be delighted if Pete and Kerry were photographed in some sun-dappled location with a batch of adorable children in tow. Nor could she have been pleased about Kerry's recent weight loss (three stone) and the fact that she was now a size eight: 'Exercise and divorce!' trilled Kerry, when asked how she managed it. 'I'm on a divorce diet! It's a whole new me. I got a bit lost in the last few years but my life's back on track now. I love my kebabs and curries, but I try to stick to salads now.'

The influence of Claire Powell didn't hurt either: under her expert guidance, Kerry was looking better than she ever had done in her life.

She was certainly looking pretty amazing these

days. So too was Pete, whose toned and tanned physique had been photographed regularly when he was in Dubai. Intensive speculation continued as to the state of his love life, with other stars hinting that he was seeing someone: 'In a magazine last week, Liz McClarnon apparently said that she knows for a fact that I've got a girlfriend!' said Pete rather wearily. 'Er, I haven't actually seen Liz for years, so I had no idea what she was going on about. I actually got someone I know to call Liz and ask if she had actually said that, and she said she didn't. I can assure you that I absolutely haven't got a girlfriend at the moment. I think someone has been telling porkies!'

But it didn't stop all the speculation, though. Pete was a good-looking bloke, single and back on the market. He was spending a lot of time with Kerry – albeit just as friends – who was also attractive and single again. His ex-wife, meanwhile, was the subject of increasingly fevered speculation. Just what would Katie Price – and not forgetting her new husband Alex Reid – do next?

CHAPTER NINE
THE PRICE OF FAME

Katie was used to negative publicity, which was fortunate: the drama surrounding Katie and Alex, and Pete and Kerry had reached boiling point and while there was no question about the fact that Katie was still the object of greatest fascination, equally she was by far the most controversial of the four. Quite how much became clear when a survey polled the British public to see who they would most like to see put in the stocks and pelt with rotten tomatoes: Katie, with 30 per cent of the vote, came a clear first, ahead of even the nation's most hated love cheat, Ashley Cole (21 per cent), and then Simon Cowell (15 per cent.) At least they noticed her. Like her or loathe her, Katie Price certainly had made her mark.

Nothing the four did went unnoticed. It was reported that Alex injected himself in the stomach with Melanotan, which is what gave him his deep tan: but there were medical voices advising caution. 'It may give you a nice tan at the moment, but we don't know what kind of long-term effects it could have,' warned Florence Palmer of the Medicines and Healthcare Products Regulatory Service. Given that Alex was a fighter, there were a fair few health hazards associated with his work, but this was clearly just one more of them.

But Katie and Alex's tans actually became a talking point. In Blackburn, a campaign by cider makers Blackthorn asked drinkers about the subjects most likely to put them off the booze: one featured a picture of Katie and Alex, with the legend, 'Disturbed by dodgy tans?' Other potential irritations included footballers who dive, bad refereeing decisions and political correctness. But Katie was not amused: 'Katie is fuming,' said a source. 'This really is her worst nightmare. She hates being called irritating and annoying.'

The good people at Blackthorn remained unrepentant, however: 'There's a lot of wisdom to be found in pubs,' said Blackthorn master cider maker Bob Cork. 'They are places where men feel comfortable expressing their views on the way they see things.

Hopefully these new findings will start even more debates over pints in pubs across Britain tonight.'

Alex minded, too. Something else he was having to come to terms with, more usually an issue for women, was the fact that he was now constantly judged on his looks – and he didn't like it one bit. Just like his paramour, he had to make sure he looked perfect at all times and like her, he was subject to extremely negative comment when he didn't. It was yet another aspect of his new life that he had to get used to.

One journalist asked him if he was vain: 'Who isn't?' Alex replied. 'We all want to look good. People see it as a negative quality. It's not! Yes, I'm very vain. I want to look good. I don't want to be called "Mr Potato Head", or "Craggy Builder"or "Monkey Boy". Which is what I am called in the press. Exactly! You're laughing! I laugh. It is hilarious. There was a picture of me [in the *Sun*] as Mr Potato Head. But the only thing is, I can't go out of the house without looking half-decent. That's one of the things about this fame that I don't like.'

Indeed, there was quite a bit that was proving to be a trial.

There had been more reports of trouble on the honeymoon, too. It emerged that Alex had booked a scuba diving course for Katie (clearly unaware of the threat of exploding breast implants), something that

Katie hadn't appreciated at all. She didn't like putting her head underwater and had expected him to know that.

Then they were back to the paranormal: Sally Morgan had been round to nose out spirits and now it was the turn of the astrologer Russell Grant. He sensed the presence of a nurse who wanted to help Harvey: 'I saw a woman in a white nurse's uniform,' he explained. 'There is absolutely no doubt to me that she was an angel. I had a dream that night and when I woke up, I knew I had got through. This woman was sacked from the building or it was sold. She was being forced out, but she didn't want to leave. When she died, she went back to this place she called her heaven. I have no doubt she is not a harmful spirit. She is bringing healing and wants to help look after her son.'

It was a measure of the massive interest in Katie that it wasn't just the public who had opinions about her: her fellow celebrities did, too. Whether or not Amanda Holden wanted to put Katie in the stocks and throw rotten tomatoes at her she wasn't saying, but she certainly had her own views on the marriage that everyone was talking about. 'I think Katie's rushed into her second marriage,' she said. 'After a long-term relationship you need to be on your own to get to know yourself again. Alex is sweet, but he's out of his depth. Katie needs a man who can handle her feisty nature.'

There were clearly some stresses behind the scenes. These may or may not have played a part in Alex's decision not to attend the première of his film *Killer Bitch* (*Babe*), about which a good deal of fuss had been made once it emerged that the movie contained a rape scene: certainly it was a surprising decision for someone who had wanted to be an actor for so long. It might have been a last-minute decision, too, for he and Katie were actually near the Curzon cinema in Mayfair where the première took place – at the Mayfair Hotel.

Co-star Yvette Rowland was left to pose with a cardboard cutout of Alex in suitable sweaty, fighting pose. If truth be told, the film was a straight-to-DVD flick about a woman who has to kill five people to save her own family from being slaughtered, but even so, Alex's absence was commented upon.

It was not clear what had made him decide to stay away. Perhaps it was a row with the missus, but equally well, Alex might have been aware that at least one visitor to the première wore a T-shirt bearing the legend, 'Alex Reid bottled it!' Some took this to be a reference to his non-appearance at the première, but really, it was of course a reference to his cancelled fight. The match had been arranged, but even so Alex's future was far from clear, not least because he himself didn't appear to know what he wanted to do.

Still, a range of controversial attendees made up for it. Former underworld figure Dave Courtney was there, as was erstwhile hooligan Cass Pennant and ex-jewel thief Lenny Hamilton. Then there was the former bareknuckle boxer Roy Shaw, while glamour was provided by the actress Jessica Bast and model Camilla Quance. The Kray twins' driver, Billy Frost, put in an appearance, too. Former drug runner Howard Marks had been invited – but was unavoidably detained elsewhere.

Alex's non-appearance, though, did nothing to staunch the rumours that he was finding it increasingly difficult to cope. It takes a certain type of personality to deal with that level of fame, especially when it appears out of the blue. Things were not looking that good for Alex and it was particularly sad because he had finally got what he wanted – but was discovering that it wasn't quite so much fun as it looked. 'The wheels are coming off for Alex, day by day. He is like Jekyll and Hyde,' said a source. 'He used to be a calm, mild-mannered mate, who was easy to be around. Now he is uncontrollable and like a wildman.'

Another friend was equally concerned. 'Alex has wanted to be famous for years and years, and did everything he could to make it,' he stated. 'But now he has everything he wished for and it is not quite the reality he was expecting. He is followed everywhere because of who his wife is and is too naive to play the game in the way that she does. The way it's going, his career will be over before it's even begun.'

In the event, it was possibly just as well that he didn't turn up. Alex was called upon to have 'rough sex' with Yvette's character, the murderess, and apparently the sounds he made were a little odd: 'The whole cinema was giggling throughout the sex scene,' said one member of the audience. 'The growls Alex makes during sex were hilarious and weird. Most people couldn't stop laughing. If that's what Jordan has to listen to in bed then she must have a good sense of humour!'

Nor did it help when Yvette's character was asked if she knew any cross dressers: 'Yeah, I do, actually,' she replies. 'But if you book him, he's unlikely to turn up.'

In the midst of all of this, Pete was still concerned with family responsibilities – not just his children, but his parents, too His father Savvas had been in ill health for some time now and so Pete arranged for both parents to fly to his villa in Cyprus, where he was able to spend some time with them.

'Pete has been working so hard, he's missed spending

time with his family,' said a source. 'His mum and dad live in Australia, so it's hard for him to see them as much as he would like. So, to make sure they are closer to home, he's flying them to Cyprus where he can visit them as often as he likes. His dad Savvas has struggled with his health in the past and he was too ill to fly over last year, so the family plan to make up for lost time. Pete is a real family man and hates his parents being so far away. He also wants them to spend quality time with his kids, Junior and Princess.'

Indeed, shortly afterwards Pete's parents flew on to London, where they were greeted rapturously at Heathrow by a beaming Pete and Princess.

Whatever was going on behind the scenes – and stocks-related public wishes notwithstanding, however – Katie's pulling power when it came to endorsements was as strong as ever. She was in talks with Toys R Us to design a range of pony-related toys to come out for the Christmas market – a very obvious extension of her brand, given that she was known to be besotted with horses and already had an equestrian range for little girls. 'The designs are at an early stage,' said a source close to the deal. 'But it's thought that there will be little ponies and lots of accessories of the kind that young girls love. There may also be models of Katie to ride the ponies, although that hasn't been decided just yet. I'm sure that the colour pink – Katie's favourite –

will feature very highly in the range. Katie loved that sort of thing as a kid and as she has grown up, she has got into riding her own horses. She really wants to inspire a whole generation to do the same as her.'

Toys R Us was an excellent company to be working with, too. They had 76 stores in the UK and 700 worldwide, which could well lead to giving Katie the international exposure that she so craved. 'These guys have a history of making big successes from most of the things they do,' continued the source. 'That's why the stores do so well. Girls across the world love ponies, so it's not hard to see why there could be worldwide popularity.'

It was all grist to the mill.

But someone else was also assiduously courting the public herself these days and she wasn't able to stay silent for long. Kerry Katona had never had quite the pulling power of Katie, but she wasn't far behind and had something to say for herself as well. Just like Katie, she was keen on having more children and overwhelmed by the sharp move upwards that her life had taken in recent weeks.

'I definitely want more children,' she declared. 'I'm an only child myself and I've always wanted a big family. I want to get divorced first and get the house sorted and then I'll be thinking about adding another to my family. I hope my future does include more kids but I'm only 29, so not straight away.'

Who would be the father? It was the million-dollar question, but Kerry was an old pro when it came to playing the media – yet another element that she shared with Katie – and she certainly wasn't going to be drawn on that one. 'I'm divorced twice already – it's not looking good, is it really?' she continued. 'I've not seen any men that have taken my fancy yet, but I'm not really looking. I need to concentrate on myself for a while. I'm actually really scared about letting another man into my life. I think it's going to take me a little while before I can trust again. I'm just concentrating on being with the kids at the moment – they're brilliant, I love spending time with them. My mum's been visiting, so it's lovely for us all to be able to spend time with each other.'

She had also learned the value of the public apology. Kerry had been a golden girl who appeared to throw it all away, and she understood that to be given a second chance, she had to make some kind of public penance for the way she'd behaved in the recent past. And so she did. 'I got a bit lost over the last few years, but my life is definitely back on track now,' she said. 'Everyone has been so nice. The public support has been amazing. I'm still feeling ashamed and embarrassed about everything that's come out over the last few years. Some of the stuff has been pretty humiliating, but I've had so much support and positive comments from people. Just knowing that everyone wants me to succeed has really lifted my spirits – and I have no intention of letting everyone down.'

No mention was made of her rival, but the elements of further tensions were there, in this case as far as the children were concerned. Katie had wanted to send hers to the Hawthorns School, the best private school in the area, but was unable to do so as the headmaster was concerned about the ensuing publicity and all the disruption it might cause. However, Kerry's brood was awarded places.

'The two older girls started last week and they absolutely love it,' said a source. 'Kerry sorted out the places before she moved down – it was her top priority. Little Heidi has just started there too but is only doing a couple of days a week as she's still very young. Kerry loves her new life – it was a big thing for her to move down to Surrey but she knew it was the only way she was going to get the fresh start she so desperately needed. And she hasn't looked back since.'

Indeed, it seemed she really had turned over a whole new leaf. 'She has a gym in her house and is up at dawn, working out,' the source continued. 'She's got acres of land and uses the hills behind her house to run up as part of her exercise regime. She looks the way she does now because of hard work and determination. She's doing it properly and the results are there for all to see – she looks amazing and feels amazing. The fact her relationship with mum Sue is back on track has also helped her feel good; Kerry believes everyone deserves a second chance and she's just so grateful that the public have given her one.'

Kerry continued to garner public sympathy with her other woes, as well. Now that she had finally gathered up the strength to part from husband Mark Croft, the house in Cheshire had been locked up, as both parties decided what to do about the future.

Mark had, in fact, been pictured at the house the previous week and was said to have commented, 'She has cleaned me out,' when he saw all the possessions Kerry had moved from the house (although given the fact that he had talked about spending Kerry's money during their time together, it is perhaps a little understandable that his wife felt fully justified in taking what she wanted for her new house.) Public sympathy was totally with her – in everyone's view she hadn't got out of that marriage a moment too soon.

Meanwhile, Katie and Alex soldiered on. Harking back to the Kirstie Allsopp remarks, Alex again showed that he was tired of being the subject of so much criticism: in his magazine column he wrote, 'Who's Kirstie Allsopp and why is she slagging off my wife? What motivated her to criticise how Katie brings up the kids? I really don't understand why Katie gets those criticisms. If she was referring to the modelling, I say why shouldn't they do that? I don't see any problem in it whatsoever. It seems anytime someone wants a front page these days, they just take a pop at Katie or me. If you have nothing nice to say, say nothing at all.'

Pete, although circumspect, clearly found it hard to see Alex taking on the role of father to his children. Unlike Alex, he was not happy at all about what was going on with the children, especially when Princess turned up on websites such as social networking site Facebook wearing make-up, which had happened in the past. 'The children only need one dad and Pete's a very constant father figure in their lives,' a friend commented. 'But Alex is married to Kate and there's nothing Pete can do about it. His concern is the kids are not made to do anything they don't want to do. If things are put up on websites for all to see, that's when he gets a bit funny about it.'

But the attention was constant and unyielding. Alex had tired of it, however. Essentially a decent man, if not the world's brainiest, he simply couldn't understand why he and Katie had become such targets: neither of them wished anyone ill. Besotted as he was by his new spouse, he just couldn't see how she was able to rub people up the wrong way. Amanda Holden was right to call her 'fiery': Katie had a mouth on her and she just couldn't help piping up when on occasion it would have been much wiser, or at least more tactful, to pipe down.

Meanwhile, it was also time for Pete's weekly magazine column and he, too, harked back to events of several days previously. In this case, he was still smarting from the reports that he had not, in fact, been asked to appear on the Australian version of the *X Factor* and wished to set the record straight.

'The fact is that Fremantle, the company that co-produces the show in Australia, sent my manager Claire Powell an email to ask me if I'd be interested in joining the show about three weeks ago – I saw it with my own eyes,' he wrote. 'Why would I feel the need to make something like this up? It's so weird when people will do anything to try and make you look stupid when all I was doing was telling the truth.

'Every week Claire and I sit down and I look at all the projects I've been asked to get involved in, and we work out what's possible and what's not. I wish I'd never mentioned it now!'

Indeed, it was all something of a mystery but at least Pete had got that one off his chest now.

Kerry had something to get off her chest, too, and it involved Katie. For some time, she had been pretty quiet on the subject but now, glowing with health and happiness, a new life in the offing and her children attending the area's best school, she decided to be magnanimous. 'I feel sorry for her,' Kerry declared. 'I feel like I'm watching some of my old life. No one knows what goes on behind closed doors. She can sit there and say: "I'm happy and really in love." But I did all that myself – you're in denial. She's not doing herself any favours, like I wasn't. I wish I'd got counselling. You suffer rejection when someone leaves you, like leaving her and Brian leaving me.'

Kerry must have known exactly what she was doing. Possibly the worst emotion to inspire in others is pity, especially when it comes to someone as proud as Katie, and for Kerry of all people to express such thoughts was almost too much. It was as if she was spoiling for a fight: first she was on Team Pete and now she was feeling sorry for Katie, who in turn must have been spitting tacks. But this was her long-awaited revenge for Katie had voiced exactly the same sentiments when Kerry had been declared bankrupt, saying something along the lines of, 'I feel sorry for her, but you shouldn't spend money when you haven't got it.' If revenge was a dish best served cold, then this one was icy:

Nor was that the full extent of her vitriol. 'Hopefully, when Pete's got a free weekend, we can take the kids to the beach,' mused Kerry. She was 'sexually frustrated' since splitting from Mark, she added, saying, 'Peter's a sweetheart, the ideal candidate, but we're friends and that we will stay.' Had she gone out of her way to find something to annoy Katie, she couldn't have done better – as Kerry must have known.

According to some reports, however, Katie had something else on her mind. Unlikely as it seemed, it appeared that she might be hoping for a reunion with Pete. According to some people, the two of them were getting on a bit better – with Katie hoping this might lead to something more. Pete's recent change of address meant that he was now closer to the children – and that meant he was closer to their mother, too.

'Jordan's so happy that things are better with her and Pete, and there's a worry that she may be getting a bit carried away,' said a source. 'His main motivation for moving closer to her home is so he can spend less time commuting to see his kids. His new home's also closer to Junior's school, so it's not about seeing more of Katie.'

It was a pretty unlikely prospect, however. Apart from the fact that Katie actually had a new husband now, there had been so much bitterness between the two of them and so much bad feeling that it was a major breakthrough that they could even exchange a few civil words. And much as Katie might have wanted it, nothing was going to change that.

CHAPTER TEN
THE FEUDING
CONTINUES

Time went on: the players in this extraordinary drama continued to move further on with their lives, planning their futures and working out what tomorrow might bring. It was beginning to look as if Pete's future might lie in television – his name had come up in connection with a new panel show to be called *Odd One In*. He had already lost his musical career once before and wanted to be fully prepared, if it happened again, this time around. And Pete was a television natural – he was not only photogenic, but had an easy-going charm that came across very well on the screen, on top of which, of course, he was an enormously popular figure and very well loved. People trusted him and they were all rooting for him; it seemed like the obvious next step.

Having a baby with Alex was still at the forefront of Katie's mind, so much so that she was even prepared to sacrifice her beloved Botox in the quest to be with child. She went along for a regular injection, but left without having had the treatment when she discovered that it could cause problems in the future: 'Katie was gutted but she didn't want to take any chances,' said a source. 'She was the one who asked whether it was safe to have the injections when pregnant. When the doctor said it wasn't advisable, Katie said, "No way." Instead she had a massage and a normal facial for an hour and a half.

'She is desperate for a baby after coming off the Pill at Christmas. She keeps saying she is worried she will have loads of wrinkles at her birthday party but deep down, all she wants is to get pregnant, so vanity has to be put to one side.'

There were many reasons why Katie wanted to have a baby with Alex, but one of them might well have been to make her feel more secure. After all, her first husband had left her and whatever the true nature of her feelings for him, Katie must have feared that it might happen again. A baby would bind the two of them in a way that nothing else could, just as it had done with her and Pete, for whatever Pete's feelings about his ex-wife, they were together in perpetuity, courtesy of the children – that, of course, and their never-ending battle to see who would finally get the upper hand.

Given how determined she was to have a baby – and how little a secret she was making of it – it was surprising when Katie caused comment by appearing in public without her wedding ring, not least because she was also sporting a T-shirt with an image of herself weeping on it. Was this some sort of subliminal message and if so, to whom? Katie was a past master at the art of expressing herself through her appearance – no one understood more fully the power of the image than she did – and if she was trying to tell the world something, this would have been in typical style.

However, the rumours that she wanted to get back with Pete were dealt a blow when it emerged that she had listed a number of items that had once belonged to them both on eBay, the internet auction site, a move that would shortly cause yet another row. Alongside some of her own outfits, she put two canvas pictures of the couple up for sale, plus a clock engraved with their names: she appeared to be wanting to make a fresh start. Besides, the time was fast approaching when she and Alex would celebrate their summer blessing – which might have been one reason why there had been an increase in the rows between them, given the strain these ceremonies bring in their wake. It was time, as she herself liked to put it, for them all to move on.

But they were inevitable, and everyone involved simply had to learn to take it on the chin. It was hard to escape the conclusion, though, that Alex worried that he was not always up to scratch, both as far as Katie and the public were concerned. Pete was a much-loved figure and though the public mood towards Alex had softened considerably in recent months, he had a way to go before achieving national treasure status, à la Pete.

Alex was still coming to terms with his new life. He had been really smarting about the criticism of *Killer Bitch* – as expected, it had received dire reviews (and that's when it was commented on at all) – and the ribbing when he didn't turn up to the première also hit home. At last he spoke out: 'It seemed like a fun idea and a way to practise my acting,' he wrote in his magazine column. 'But I wasn't with Katie when I signed up, so I hadn't realised the attention it would get.'

It certainly did get that: above all, the most notorious sex scene in the film, which was commented on and condemned, over and over again. 'For the last time, it's not a rape scene – it's a love scene!' insisted

Alex. 'And there was no problem for Katie when I did that scene. Sadly, I think some of the people involved in the film just used me to get publicity.' That might well have been the case, but it was something that Alex would have to get used to – and fast. As so often is the case, Alex was beginning to realise the fame he had wanted so very badly came at a heavy price. Was it one that he considered worth paying, though? Yes – for now.

But he certainly wasn't the wide-eyed innocent he'd been until just eight months previously, when he and Katie first met. Because he doesn't look like the sort of boy who would still live within the protective environment of his parents' home, even though he was in his mid-thirties and a big, mean cage-fighter, it was easy to forget that that's exactly what he once was. Alex had gone from that extremely tight-knit unit into the company of an incredibly competitive woman, who liked to engage in power games with her men. Naturally, it was bound to have been something of a shock.

Several of Katie's feuds came home to roost in early May. On one eventful day, she headed for the Mayfair Hotel (the same one where she'd taken sanctuary when she and Alex missed the première of his film a week previously and a favourite when she was in London) for a business meeting only to discover on arrival that the magazine *Attitude* was hosting a party that evening. Until relatively recently, Katie and *Attitude* had been great buddies – when she'd put a stop to the photoshoot that the magazine was doing with Alex – and since then relations had been a little chilled.

It was not exactly clear what had happened as far as the party itself was concerned, but what appeared to be the case was that while the magazine had not invited her, the hotel had. 'She had a face like thunder,' said one observer. 'She stormed past the door pretending not to notice what was going on, but she didn't convince anyone.'

Worse, however, far worse, was that Kerry Katona had been invited – and indeed, was already there. Was this the real reason why Katie hadn't been asked? 'We heard Katie was fuming over that comment [by *Attitude* editor Matthew Todd, who said she'd destroyed the photoshoot]. Since she and Kerry can be volatile, it didn't seem a good idea to put them in the same room,' revealed a source. In actual fact, both had been photographed coming and going from the hotel premises earlier in the day and had only just missed each other. What might have happened, had they met, hardly bears thinking about, for with all the growing tensions, there had been no contact between them for years – not that

that stopped the ever-increasing rivalry between the two women.

Indeed, both were increasingly sought-after at the capital's celebrity events, both guaranteed to maximise coverage, create copy and spark the public's interest, and so it was inevitable that they would one day clash over events – but to choose Kerry over her? Other than a man doing so, it is difficult to imagine a scenario that Katie would hate more. 'We did not invite Katie Price, but the hotel organisers asked her along without realising about our little spat,' said Matthew Todd. 'I believe she was there in the day, having meetings. We would have happily invited her ourselves, however, if she would apologise for ruining our photoshoot with Alex Reid.'

Whatever the scenario, Katie was absolutely livid – and walked out.

Not so Phil Turner and Gary Cockerill, however, her two great friends who had turned up with her and decided (although not officially invited) that they would stay in situ and party on. At least that way they could give Katie all the gossip about the bash that she herself was obliged to miss.

'Katie stormed off when she realised Kerry was inside,' said one observer at the scene. '...Kerry's people were like guarddogs protecting her. I think they were worried about it turning into a bitch fight in the middle of the dance floor. Kerry just got on with it, and looked like she was having a great time and she was very well behaved.'

Of course, it was in her best interests to do so. Kerry was thoroughly enjoying this new and happier stage of her life – she certainly didn't want it crashing down around her ears. A public spat with Katie would have looked down-market and trashy, two words much-associated with Kerry in recent years, which she was now desperate to get away from. If this was to be her second chance then she'd have to learn to behave, even in exceedingly trying situations.

She herself wasn't doing anything to calm matters down, though. Her last proclamation on the subject of Katie's ex ran thus: 'Pete is the ideal candidate and definitely boyfriend material. I can see why women love Pete. He's the perfect guy to take home to your mum. He's everything a girl needs.' It was hardly the sort of remark to soothe Katie, or pour oil on troubled waters. Indeed, it sometimes seemed as if Kerry was thoroughly enjoying upsetting her rival and if you didn't take it too seriously (which Katie unfortunately did), why not? Very wisely, Kerry had not gone so far as to make any barbed remarks about Katie personally: she was just getting her point across that she was back on the scene and Katie wasn't the only show in town.

And Katie was beginning to reveal that it riled her. Kerry, probably guided by her manager Claire, was playing a very clever game: she was able to engage with Katie without saying anything directly about her. The only remarks she ever made were positive – and about Pete. The fact that she knew the effect this would have was neither here nor there: it had the result of making her look good-hearted, in praising Pete, and at the same time gave the impression that she hadn't actually noticed Katie was around at all. For someone usually so good at playing the media, Katie was getting it all wrong: instead of just rising above it, she continued to make very barbed remarks indeed directly about Kerry, which had the effect of making herself look both jealous and mean-spirited.

As Kerry's recovery continued apace, it began to look as if she really might be able to once more recoup her role as the nation's sweetheart. Now that Kerry had seen the error of her ways she was very much being welcomed back into the fold. And like Katie, she was having to face all the difficult issues regarding access to the children that so many divorcing couples experience, although in her case the problems were particularly acute.

At least Katie and Pete hadn't both gone for sole access: there was some realisation that it was probably best if the children lived with Katie while having as much access as possible to Pete. But this was not the case where Kerry was concerned: it seemed Mark planned to go for sole access, complaining that because Kerry had moved down south it had made matters difficult for him.

'They are going to fight each other to the bitter end,' said a source. 'Kerry says they should be with her because she is their mother. Mark says he's going to remind the court of every single time Kerry praised him as a father.'

The court hearings were just beginning – yet another painful and ugly part of the process of Kerry putting her life back together but again, a necessary duty that had to be done. Perhaps not surprisingly, the early stages went well for Kerry and she left court looking a lot more cheerful than she had when she arrived. 'Kerry was delighted with how the case went yesterday,' said a friend. 'She thinks the judge was very sympathetic towards her.'

It was hardly a shock, given recent events, and Kerry was now clearly determined to make a fresh start. Again she appeared to be having an even worse time than Katie, though, because while Katie had only one ex-husband to deal with, Kerry now had two. Brian McFadden had also muttered about going for custody of his two children, which seemed an equally unlikely prospect given that he'd been living on the other side of the world for some years now, but Kerry was gaining in courage and confidence all the time.

Although Mark was not engaged anything like so closely as his estranged wife in all the shenanigans surrounding Katie, Alex and Pete, he was still doing his bit to draw the public in. Whether Katie wanted her there or not, Kerry had become part of the Katie and Pete saga and so her whole story, plus the troubles she was now experiencing somehow impacted on what was going on with her new neighbours up the road. Clearly, she was having a hard time of it with Mark but was fighting back so bravely and it reflected well on Pete that he had offered a shoulder for her to cry on. But it was not just the rivalry between Kerry and Katie that intrigued – it was the role she was playing in Pete's life – and vice versa, too.

CHAPTER ELEVEN

ACTING MAN OR FIGHTING MAN?

In the meantime, there was still a lot of intense interest in Alex's appearance. There had been all those stories about tanning injections, as well as speculation that Katie was trying to turn him into a second version of Pete, looks-wise at least. In fact, Alex was quite touchingly open on the subject and even sounded a little hurt about all the fuss. It was another instance of the downside of fame, but now he really did have to get used to it.

'I like to look good and wear nice clothes, but I've just had a crew cut at the gym!' he explained. 'As for the tanning injections, yes I've had them, but I thoroughly researched them first and I haven't had one for ages. I actually read that they have anti-carcinogenic properties. I'm into health. It's like anything – if you have a glass of wine a day, that's fine, but 20 glasses isn't! I don't like that dark tanned look that I had on *Big Brother*, anyway – I prefer the natural look.' He still appeared staggered that such attention was coming his way – and even had to deny that he was addicted to beauty treatments. (The same, of course, could not be said for his wife.)

Indeed, one of the problems that Alex had was a strong feeling that he was being tarred with the same brush as his wife. Because Katie was so well known when they met and Alex was a completely unknown quantity, people tended to assume that their likes and dislikes were the same. If Katie spent her entire time having beauty treatments, then in an illogical but understandable fashion, people tended to think the same of her spouse. Nor were matters helped by the fact that Alex seemed to be so very much under his wife's spell these days: even if he hadn't been like her when they first met, their tastes were increasingly closely associated because she had so much say in everything they did.

Still, things was looking up: both continued to be very much sought-after and in demand. Katie's controversial jaunt to Ibiza the previous summer had caused a good deal of tut-tutting at the time, not least from Pete, but it had the unexpected benefit of raising her profile enormously in Spain. She still wanted to be a global name rather than just one based in the UK, and courtesy of her wild gallivanting, she had that particular country eating out of her hand. A combination of outrageous clothing, far too much drinking, even more outrageous behaviour and a furious husband (as he still was) back home, all combined to intrigue.

'People in Spain knew about Jordan when she was married to Peter Andre but she was never really a big star,' said a source. 'But last year in Ibiza she really came to the attention of the country's big players. Journalists and TV producers in the major cities finally saw the mileage in her. There is even talk of one of the TV stations buying up her reality series and that could be a major hit. They are hoping she will become one of Spain's most popular celebs – and it's all thanks to that wild bender in Ibiza.' But then it should have been no surprise – Katie's life was also her career, and had been for many years now. There was also talk of some of her novels being published in Spain.

With perfect timing, it was announced that Katie would make a guest appearance in *Benidorm*, alongside another old trooper, Cilla Black. Derren Litten, the writer and creator of the show, made the announcement (rather ironically at a party held by

Attitude): 'Both women are great signings for the show and I can't wait to work with them,' he said. 'Cilla has basically agreed to play the oldest swinger in town and will really ham it up in a basque and suspenders, all the works. The show will be going out in the autumn and will be very special. I'm really proud of it. I've always wanted to work with Katie too, so we've been in touch with her people and offered her a role playing a completely chavvy Brit abroad, getting them out for the lads and lying by the pool. She probably won't have to do too much acting – it will be more sunbathing and bikini action.' Indeed – the initial run-through had been held the summer before.

And so all the dire predictions about Katie's very-public lurch back into her Jordan persona the previous summer were wide of the mark: if anything, it had helped her career. She was now an extremely rich woman in her own right and becoming all the more so: although as ambitious as ever, she had long since passed the stage where she actually needed to work. Rather, she continued to do so partly because she really did want to become globally famous and partly, funnily enough, because she had – and still has – a strong work ethic and frankly, would have considered it wrong to stop now.

For all the criticism levelled at Katie over the years,

it has sometimes been forgotten that she pulled herself up from nothing and went on to make a huge name for herself without any help from anyone else. She is a totally self-made woman, who has never asked for any handouts, never required that her men support her and has never at any time – even after the birth of Harvey, when she discovered the full extent of his health problems or her divorce from Pete – ever given in to self-pity. There are many ways in which she continues to be an admirable role model, whatever the naysayers might say.

But her driving habits were not one of them. Katie had possibly the most noticeable horsebox in the country, painted a vivid shade of pink, and it was while driving this particular statement that she was spotted by the police talking on her mobile phone. 'The officers who pulled Jordan over in the horsebox could hardly believe their eyes,' said a source. 'There was not much trouble identifying the driver – and the horsebox isn't exactly subtle.'

'A 31-year-old woman has been summoned to appear at Crawley Magistrates on two different occasions for offences relating to not being in proper control of a motor vehicle and excess speed,' said a spokesman for Sussex Police.

It was, in fact, a bit of a blow. Katie promptly enlisted the services of Nick Freeman, also known as

'Mr Loophole' for his astounding ability to get very famous celebrities off scot-free when caught well over the speed limit, and she needed him, too. Already she had three penalty points on her licence, something she did not wish to lose: an avid rider like Katie needed to be able to get about and keep her licence intact.

Alex continued to grumble at his critics – almost invariably, alas, saying the wrong thing. The controversial scene at the heart of *Killer Bitch* continued to haunt him and he defended it yet again, this time, unfortunately, managing to compare himself to one of the greatest actors alive today. 'I just wish that people would realise that scene is a love scene,' he repeated. 'I mean, Robert De Niro does love scenes and no one brands him a pervert.'

Poor Alex! Most of the time he was quite upfront in saying that he wasn't much of an actor, really – but here he seemed to be allying himself with the very best. Of course he didn't mean to do this, but he simply hadn't mastered the tricks of dealing with the press at all and so he put himself up for a fair bit of ribbing once more. Neither he nor Katie seemed to be much cop at rising above it all at the time, but to offer a hostage to fortune such as this was unfortunate indeed. Robert De Niro! Had he compared himself to Sir Laurence Olivier, it wouldn't have been more far-fetched.

As the renewal of vows – or second wedding, really – drew closer, friends of the couple noticed that Katie seemed to have taken a melancholic turn. Resigned to the fact that she and Pete really were apart and always would be, they reported that she had started to call Pete, 'the love of her life.' The fact that this latest wedding was probably not going to be a patch on the first didn't help either (indeed, the £600,000 they were receiving for it was only half the price tag of the last time around), and although Katie still intended to go ahead with it, some feared that her heart wasn't really in it anymore.

'Katie obviously has feelings for Alex, but in her eyes he will never compare to Peter, who she calls the love of her life,' said one. 'She rushed into the Vegas wedding and she and Alex both felt it would be nice to renew their vows in a traditional church service. But the nearer they get to the date, the less interested Katie becomes. She just keeps going on about when she married Pete and how it was the "perfect day". For her, it was a real-life fairytale and exactly how she'd always imagined her big day.'

Of course, it wouldn't be anything like as lavish as the first wedding, which couldn't help but matter to Katie. It was a second wedding, not a first, and even in the world of celebrity, it would simply not have been appropriate to celebrate on the same scale as before. The ceremony was to be held just over a year after the separation from Pete and considerably less than that time from the divorce: even those able to move on as fast as Katie seemed to be might have thought twice about going so totally over the top once more. Indeed, in some ways the Las Vegas ceremony, for all its surprise value, worked better within the context of this new relationship because it had been spontaneous (up to a point) – and simple. And they were, after all, now wed.

But the blessing was bringing home the reality of what had happened over the last year, for even now many people believed Katie was still in denial about the split. The fact that she was not only getting married again, but setting up the whole accompanying palaver really brought it home to her – and the fact that Pete now lived closer to her than he had done previously just made things a whole lot worse. When he was further away, it was easier to forget about the life they'd once shared, but now they were almost neighbours (with Kerry in the vicinity, as well), it was a lot harder to turn away from the past.

Indeed, some people were beginning to describe Katie's feelings towards Pete as 'fairly worrying.' There were reports that she constantly asked the children: 'Who is with Daddy?' when they spent time with Pete and that she was having her staff drive by his new place so that she could find out what was going on. They were not the actions of a woman who has got over her ex and is madly in love with someone else.

And Pete did not return the sentiment. Rather, as Katie and Alex's wedding approached, he was at pains to lay down his feelings about Kerry again. 'Kerry Katona said in an interview last week that I was her ideal man, but that she doesn't want to burden me too much with her problems,' he wrote. 'I love Kerry and will always be there for her as a friend and she is more than welcome to call me whenever she needs to talk. I would never see her as a burden. I am so impressed with the way she is turning her life around, as it can't be easy for her.'

He then turned to the subject of Katie, though not in a good way. It turned out that he had been horrified when he discovered that she had put some goods relating to both of them up for auction on eBay and indeed, to have done so wasn't like her at all. Katie's management of the media was usually often nothing less than superb: after years in the spotlight, no one was better at knowing what played well with whom. It was mystifying, therefore, that she'd done something that was bound to reflect badly on her. Pete was not pleased: 'As you may or may not have heard, my ex-wife took it upon herself to sell old family pictures of ours on eBay last week,' he said. 'I am dealing with this matter privately and don't want to say too much, but I will admit that I wasn't exactly delighted when I found out about it!'

And so the feuding festered on. Katie's forthcoming nuptials might at least have provided grounds for some kind of peace talks between the pair, with both rising to the occasion and wishing one another well – in reality, of course, they did nothing of the sort.

CHAPTER TWELVE

KATIE AND ALEX – AND KERRY AND PETE

As Katie and Pete went public with their row over the items that Katie had put up for sale on eBay, Kerry also suffered problems on the home front. One downside to being so publicly happy in her new home was that the entire country knew that the old one was empty, and so perhaps it was inevitable that burglars made their way in, trashed the place and took irreplaceable objects as far as sentimental value was concerned, as well as everything else.

'Kerry is absolutely heartbroken,' said her mother. 'She can't believe someone could do this to her – it's just disgusting. Kerry was in floods of tears when she found out. She was at my house on the phone to her friend and I just heard her start bawling. Now the children haven't got a television to watch and all her memorabilia from when she was in Atomic Kitten and the Jungle has been smashed up.

'She had a lot of things in frames that she really treasured and they were just smashed all over the place. The thing that upset her most was the piano. Molly loves sitting there, playing on it and writing songs.'

Nor were her problems with Brian completely over: 'Kerry lives in a fantasy world,' he fumed. 'It's all absolute nonsense. She was making it up as she went along and didn't care how hurtful she was being. I don't know why she said I only ring the girls five times a year. It can be difficult because of the time difference – when the girls wake up, it's the middle of the night here but I ring my girls twice a week. I was upset and furious at Kerry's claims. It came out of the blue. I thought all that stupid war of words was behind us. She obviously did it to justify the amount of money she was being paid to do the interview.'

Sympathy, however, remained firmly on Kerry's side.

But Katie was polarising opinion as much as ever and others in the world of celebrity continued to have their say. The latest to do so was the hirsute television presenter Justin Lee Collins: he had been lined up for a new chat show on Channel 5 (hadn't everyone?) and was asked whether it was true that he'd say that he wouldn't want Katie on the programme.

'Yes, there is some truth in that,' he admitted. 'I was asked if I'd have her on and I was like, "I'm just a bit Jordan-ed out" – as I think we generally all seem to be.' But would he invite Alex? 'Absolutely! I think the reason he did well on *Celebrity Big Brother* is because there seems to be an honesty there: I want guests who are going to be honest, not ones who deliberately want to upset people or be outrageous just for the sake of it. The show is called *Good Times*, after all.'

Justin had actually said that without Pete, Katie had no filter and that appeared to be true. No one could accuse Pete of being domineering, but there was something about him that seemed to control his wife's greater excesses, and Alex had not yet developed the knack. Of course, Alex wasn't quite so much Katie's equal in celebrity terms as Pete was, which might have had something to do with it, but he didn't seem able to tone her down when she was getting to be too much. Even so, Justin might be of one opinion but the public had another: they still adored Katie and couldn't get enough of her. Besides, what was one chat show between friends?

Poor Alex, though, still had a lot to put up with. The sighting of a ring-less Katie a week earlier sent the rumour-mill into overdrive and Alex felt it was time to address that, too. Everything was fine between them, he insisted, a tad wearily: they were still as strong and as close as ever.

'I know everyone was talking about why Kate wasn't wearing her wedding ring last week on the way to the May Fair Hotel, but it doesn't mean anything,' he wrote. 'She was going to a photoshoot and didn't need it. I don't wear my wedding ring when I'm training. It seems that every little thing we do is scrutinised, but our relationship is as strong as ever. I just wish people would realise that.'

By now, he was also beginning to have some insight into the strains that might have pushed Katie and Pete apart. Some celebrities (the wise ones, many might say) keep their private lives totally separate from their public personas, so that whatever might happen out in public, at least they have a refuge to turn to in the shape of home unlike Katie and Alex. Both made a great song and dance about not living in the public eye in the way that Katie and Pete had done, but there was precious little evidence of it: indeed, the cameras appeared to be allowed to explore every angle of this new relationship quite as intimately as they had done in the past. It was a high-risk strategy for the simple reason that there was no hiding place when things went wrong. When your life is a reality TV show, what do you do when you're tired, feeling vulnerable and want to retreat into the background for a bit of peace and quiet? You suffer very publicly – and if you're really unlucky, you get slated for that, too.

As preparations for the wedding continued, all this became more of an issue. For Alex, it had happened so fast – meeting and marrying Katie within the space of a few months – that he hadn't really taken on board before then the wider implications of what they were doing. But now he'd had a taste of what life with her was really like and it was challenging, to say the least. Constantly judged on his appearance, mocked for his pretensions to acting and compared to the saintly Peter Andre, sometimes he must have wondered what he was letting himself in for. Nor was there any sign that Katie was letting up. On the contrary, her anger towards both Pete and Kerry just appeared to be growing and she was fighting back in the only way she knew how: by getting more publicity than any of them. And that meant acres of newsprint about Alex, too.

In the meantime, someone else's television career was going well. There was increasing speculation that Kerry Katona was being lined up to replace Dannii Minogue on the *X Factor* (Dannii was pregnant), speculation that the lady herself did nothing to quell. 'I'm waiting for Simon to ask me to join the *X Factor*,' she chirped. 'I think I'd be an amazing judge. I'm thinking about starting my pop career again, so the *X Factor* could be the perfect stage for that, too.'

At this rate, they would all star on one another's shows.

Indeed, life for Kerry just seemed to get better and better. She was pictured out with her 3-year-old daughter Heidi as her erstwhile road manager Carl Machin (who was single) taught her how to fish. The scene could not have been more bucolic: the three of them larked about in the Surrey countryside, with a friend commenting, 'She had never been fishing, but I said it was something that I remembered doing with my dad when I was young.'

It was a nice, relaxing break before a red carpet appearance that night in a black lace dress for the première of *The Prince of Persia: The Sands of Time* – Gemma Arterton and Jake Gyllenhaal were in attendance, but Kerry still held her own. The transformation in such a short time was extraordinary and unlike previous occasions, during which Kerry had managed to hold it together briefly before her life went pear-shaped again, this time around she didn't look like faltering. There were rumours that she missed her old life in Cheshire – scarcely surprising as it is the place where she grew up – but the change in her circumstances was such that it must have made the homesickness a little easier to bear.

It had emerged that Kerry was now working with the personal coaches Nick and Eva Speakman in a bid to restore her shattered self-confidence: 'She's been working closely with Nick and Eva again for a few weeks and they're really helping her with her issues,' said a source. 'It's not something that's going to happen overnight, but she's definitely on the right track.' Indeed, it was a lack of inner resources that had led Kerry to make such a mess of her life first time around: utterly insecure in the wake of her grim childhood, she was both a target for leeches and a very obvious candidate for depression. The determination needed to turn her life around was a big one indeed.

And her new appearance wasn't exactly hurting, either. Kerry had become terribly overweight in the past, but now she was a sleek eight and looked every inch the svelte star that she once was. 'I'm getting a lot more male attention since I lost the weight but I'm happy being single at the moment!' she told one reporter – but for how long? A stylist had been brought in to smarten up her image: Kerry was mixing high street with designer to achieve a much chicer look than she'd had in the past. She was seen browsing through gowns in the exclusive Kruszynska boutique, where the starting price for the couture on display was about £3,000. When she was spotted out and about in a very stylish statement coat by Lisa Jayne Dann, from glamboutique.co.uk, the website promptly published a picture of Kerry in the coat. Not so long ago, designers would have recoiled from being associated with the fallen star, now she was turning into their secret marketing tool.

All the while, Katie could only look on: she, too, liked to be judged on her appearance and had recently written a book on it all – *Standing Out*. But unlike Kerry, no one ever told Katie that she was looking chic and stylish. It wasn't her look – she'd never claimed it was– but that didn't mean that she relished watching Kerry turn into a clotheshorse.

Nor was life quiet on the domestic front. Katie didn't appear to have learned from past mistakes and rumours continued to surface about problems between her and Alex – again, a mirror image of issues she'd had with Pete. First, she'd been putting him down professionally, just as she had Pete in her first marriage, and now she was said not to approve of the success he was finding for himself.

This could put Alex in a very difficult position. If Alex didn't work, then he would be blamed for sponging off Katie, and if he did, he'd be accused of trading on her name. For a man not famed for his intellectual acumen, it was impossible to know what to make of it all. And what of his fighting career? The cancelled fight was still rescheduled to take place in

September, but to some observers it appeared that Alex wasn't doing anything like as much training as he needed to. Nor, with all the drama raging around him, did he have the peace and quiet to decide his next move.

And there was no one he could turn to while all this was going on, either, for there was only one man who knew exactly what it was like to be in the position he was in and that man was Peter Andre. But Alex could hardly go to ask Pete for advice. Indeed, although Pete was still doing his own reality TV shows and magazine columns among other projects, his life was noticeably calmer now. Not even kiss-and-tell stories from models he'd had flings with could begin to rival the whirlwind experience he'd had previously and he might be forgiven for being highly relieved that now it was the turn of someone else to be the focus of attention – to say nothing of being the recipient of Katie's sometimes extremely sharp tongue.

CHAPTER THIRTEEN

A PREGNANT PAUSE

Katie was desperate to become pregnant, still to no avail, and it was Alex who suggested she try yoga and meditation techniques, to some good effect. 'Katie was really sceptical at first, but after Alex Reid kept nagging, she thought, hell, why not?' said a source. 'She started with breathing exercises and yoga stretching but was soon asking Alex to teach her more advanced techniques. Not only does she now feel like a million pounds, it's bringing her and Alex closer together.'

For that was one thing that Alex had to offer that none of her other men had – expertise when it comes to health and fitness. Admittedly, Dwight Yorke, as a footballer, would have been very clued up on those subjects himself, but in celebrity terms Alex was closer to Katie's world than Dwight had ever been and was in a position to give sound advice. Better still, Alex could offer her tips on improving her appearance – and if there was one thing Katie was certain to listen to, it was that. Besides, if she got into yoga, there was always the potential for a range of yoga clothing. Business was business, after all.

Alex, in the meantime, was insistent that things between the two of them were better than ever. 'I have a deeper connection with Katie as I feel more positive influences are rubbing off on her,' he declared. That particular statement was in reference to the yoga, but life was still perking up. Now all she had to do was to become pregnant and their world would once more be perfect.

And so, serious planning began. One thing that is certain in the future is that Katie Price will remain as supremely pragmatic as she has always been. She is unashamed of the need to earn as much as she can and very good at raking in the cash. If Alex could fit in with that, then all would be just fine.

'No one can live without money,' she insisted in an interview as far back as 2008. 'Money and religion are the big things, and that's it – and I stay away from religion. We love to earn money, who doesn't? It gets you things and it's security, but at the same time it doesn't bring you good health and not always happiness. I just think Harvey is going to need to be set up for life, with his ways, and I want the other kids to have a good start in life, too.'

Of course, that was another element to it all – the children. Katie had not come from a wealthy background and she wanted to make sure that her family enjoyed all the advantages that she herself had not. Harvey, in particular, would always need the funds for special care, but Katie wanted to set her other two children up for life, as well. And if she and Alex did manage to produce their own offspring, then there would be an even larger family to make provision for – something their parents would be more than able to do.

By this stage, the sheer range of everything Katie was involved with was extraordinary: the reality shows, the magazine interviews and then the huge range of businesses and promotions just never seemed to stop. And of course, there were the books, too. But were those works to be judged simply on their covers? Katie was now a prolific novelist and author of little girls' pony tales, although in actual fact, they were just another form of promotion and the simple fact was that no one was sure whether Katie had actually ever read all of them.

'They're [the book world] not really into me and

I've got to respect it,' she said, back in 2008. 'I don't sit there and write my books and I've always said that. I'm always honest, I'm not going to bullshit people, but a lot of people do sit there and type up their books – that's what they are really good at – and then they see some glamour girl come in, who thinks she can move everyone to the side and put her name to a book although it isn't just me putting my name to the book because I do say how I want the stories and all that...'

So, did she use a Dictaphone?

'I talk into a Dictaphone and they go away and type it,' said Katie earnestly. 'I've got so many other things to do, I couldn't sit there and type, plus I didn't pass English. But ultimately I'd say there is room for everyone. It's the same with the horse world I'm into now, the dressage – you get so many snobs. That's the one thing about this country: if someone is good at something, they always try and drag them down. I love it if they try and drag me down because I'm like, watch me, I'll be more successful, and I just love it. *Love* it!'

It would be a foolhardy person who tried to drag Katie down. Of the various female rivals she'd had over the years, only Kerry was still going strong: others, such as Jodie Marsh, had disappeared off Katie's radar many years ago. There were few projects that she'd taken on that hadn't come to fruition and just about every ambition she'd ever voiced had come to pass. She had almost nothing left to prove now, yet such was the scale of her ambition that there was no chance whatsoever that she would ever stop.

Katie and Pete marked the first anniversary of their split with the usual bitterness: both said they were better off without the other, while Katie claimed she had now met, 'The love of her life.' 'Kate's life has changed dramatically in the past year,' said her spokesman. 'But having now met the love of her life in Alex [Reid], she couldn't be happier. She is now looking forward to a long and happy future with her husband and children.'

The message was clear: Pete, you're history. But it couldn't help but reveal a small mark of vulnerability – Katie Price wasn't quite the cold and unbending person she sometimes seemed to want to put across.

Pete, as usual, struck the right note in that he expressed grief, dignity and, in his case, a far more convincing assessment of his state of mind: 'Pete still cannot believe what has happened in the last year, it is a very sad situation,' said his spokesman. 'However, he is in a much, much better place than he was this time last year and ten times happier.' And that was for sure. Just as Kerry had been glowing, literally, in recent months, Pete was beginning to do the same. He was looking as good as he had done in the 'Mysterious Girl' days: he'd kept off the weight that he'd lost in the aftermath of the break-up, but there was also a spring in his step these days. Surely it wouldn't be long before the much-loved (and highly eligible) Peter Andre finally found love?

Certainly Alex's friends in the fighting community were noticing a changed man. 'Alex is under Jordan's thumb,' said fellow cage-fighter Jack Mason. 'He's as tough as they come in a fight, but the guy just doesn't look like it with all the sun beds he has. Some of the other fighters have laughed at him, especially the idea of having plastic surgery. What's the point in having your nose done if you have another fight and it happens again? You'd only want it done if your career was over!'

Indeed, that's exactly what friends feared for Alex if he didn't get his training back on schedule. Many believed that the real reason why he called off the fight was that he just wasn't fit enough and if he didn't take steps to rectify this, then it would cause him serious problems in the longer term. 'A partner should be supportive,' Jack went on. 'Not being able to train will be frustrating for Alex. I'm so grumpy when I don't train – you don't know what to do with yourself. I can't understand it with Jordan because she must work out as well and with her money, she could help him but some people are selfish. He could train with the best guys in the world, getting the best coaches in the States or wherever he wanted. Instead, he did this TV show, doing this Mickey Mouse fight stuff around the world, and you could see on his face that he was embarrassed. It was pointless. I wouldn't go near that woman! You can't expect someone to give up fighting; he hasn't been in control of all the decisions about his career.'

As for the cancelled fight – 'He says it was an injury, but you'd just go ahead anyway – that's what a fighter does. You've been training for two months and it would let everyone down to pull out over a silly little injury.'

To take on Katie Price so publicly was a big mistake, however. With her hugely competitive instinct, any form of criticism was a direct challenge and so if Alex's fellow fighters started to criticise the way she treated her husband then she was even more likely to play up, not less. In circumstances such as this, she would also expect Alex to stand up for her, whether or not he privately agreed with his old friends and so this interjection, however well meaning, was almost certain to make matters worse.

But it was almost as if a group of Alex's old friends, having seen the change in him – before and after the wedding, were making one last concerted attempt to rescue their old chum from his new life. Whether or not Alex actually wanted to be rescued was a moot point, but they may have felt that by making Katie's treatment of him a matter of public record, it would either shake him into standing up for himself, or shame Katie into behaving better. At any rate, a few of them seemed to be prepared to stand up for what they believed.

And it wasn't just the fighting. There were plenty of other reports about ructions on the home front, too. Katie was extremely good at establishing and running feuds – as Kerry might testify – but these were coming increasingly closer to home. There were stories that she was rowing with his family – not a good sign: it bears repetition that Alex lived at home until he met his wife and as such regarded it as a refuge, one that could always be returned to. It wasn't a good idea on Katie's part to push him so publicly back into the loving arms of his parents.

Indeed, Alex's mother was beginning to feel some concern about Katie's attitude towards her son. His friends felt the same way. 'She even fell out with Alex's brother Rupert because he called her a control freak, so she banned him from attending their wedding in the summer,' revealed a friend. 'But because Alex's mum was so upset, Alex put his foot down and Rupert was re-invited. He's basically had enough of Katie's constant sniping and taunts. She's always saying, "Well, Pete did this and Pete did that." After they had a screaming row last week about all the comparisons and snidey remarks, Alex threatened to call off their summer blessing because he's just reached breaking point. Katie was shocked because he's never made a stand before and it really took her by surprise. She's been punishing him for it ever since. But Alex is too scared to leave her; he'll never walk out on her.'

Or at least, she hoped not. There had already been very many similarities between Katie's first and second marriage: now there appeared to be another one, too. Pete and Alex both married someone who was, if not exactly sweet natured, certainly no more than fiery when they first got together, and in both cases that person turned into someone else. Katie seemed to delight in goading and pushing away her men once they finally married, although she might also have subconsciously been testing boundaries to see how far she could go. Too far, according to Pete, and he wasn't the only one who felt like that. It was getting to Alex and he was clearly desperate for change.

'Alex will admit to friends that the Katie he's married to now is completely different to the Katie he met eight months ago,' said a friend. 'He never knows where he stands and her cutting remarks have affected him badly. He's never felt so low, because he really loves her and it's as if he can do no right. His mum Carol is concerned for him, although his dad Bob says he's made his bed and he'd better lie in it now. To many people, his relationship with Katie seemed like a sham for a long time – the rows have turned more and more bitter, and they're so often apart. It'll be difficult for Alex if they split, not only because of losing Katie, but because of everything else he's lost. He's simply too terrified to split.'

Certainly, Alex had given up an awful lot. For all the opportunities now open to him, he was no longer entirely living life on his own terms, as he had done before. And whatever happened in the future, he would always be marked out by the time he'd spent with Katie Price. There were plenty of people who believed that the stories about cross dressing were greatly exaggerated, in order to court publicity, but come the time when Alex wanted to be taken seriously, it would always rear its head. Nor did it help that he was beginning to seem somewhat henpecked – hardly the macho look he liked to cultivate. If gentle Pete could be pushed to breaking point, then anyone could – and friends couldn't help wondering what might happen next.

As for his pals in the fighting community, they

could only hope that Katie would start to be a little more supportive. 'It can be pretty tough when you're in a relationship to do all the training you need to do in the cage-fighting world, which is four or five hours a day,' said Jack Mason, 'but my girlfriend is understanding about it because she competes in horse-riding events and she wants me to do well. I'd like to think he'll fight again. He's a bit of an idiot, but he's not a bad person. He's quite endearing, really. He's supposed to be fighting Tom Watson again in September, but he's cancelled so many fights already because of injury recently, so who knows? He's been fighting for so long, though, that I don't think he's ready to give up his old life yet.'

He probably wasn't, but events had so quickly careered out of control that Alex was forced to run to keep up with them. He had got himself into an extraordinary world, with an extraordinary woman, and that would have flummoxed a great many people with a far bigger sense of self and where they were going than Alex.

So, what would he do next? Would Katie calm down and start being supportive? And what would happen once the summer wedding took place? So much to think about – and so little seemed certain.

CHAPTER FOURTEEN
ALEX FIGHTS BACK

Funnily enough, until now the most passive member of the quartet had seemed to be Alex. Although he was the one who was the professional fighter, everyone who knew him agreed that actually, he had a certain sweetness of character, an endearing honesty that made people warm to him. Of course, this was not the way that he was in the ring, but how he was in real life. And so while Katie, Pete and Kerry all sought to manipulate the news agenda to their own advantage, Alex, to a certain extent, tended to react to events rather than set them in train himself.

Alex was also nothing like as media-savvy as the others when it came to looking after himself. He was artless and he didn't understand, sometimes, how things would sound when they came out – hence the Robert De Niro gaffe. Nor did it help that he had made a spectacularly poor choice of film in *Killer Bitch* – De Niro himself wouldn't have been able to rescue that particular vehicle, let alone someone like Alex, whose acting experience was, with the best will in the world, negligible. The timing couldn't have been worse, either – for the movie to be released at about the same time as he got together with one of Britain's most high profile women ensured a level of scrutiny that it certainly would not have received otherwise and the no-show at the première just made things worse. It had placed Alex in an unenviable position: if he showed up, the media would have gone wild, but his no-show made it look as if he was ashamed of the film – and it continued to rankle. Alex, meanwhile, did his best to clear it all up, but with only limited success.

And so, the row surrounding it all escalated. Of course, Alex had been pulled into all Katie's feuds, but this meant that he was now developing a fair few of his own. The war of words on *Killer Bitch* continued and turned increasingly rancorous: 'The guys behind *Killer Bitch* have hit out at me for saying they are using me for publicity. Of course they are!' he said, with some justification. 'I keep seeing pictures of me being used to promote the film, so that says it all. I pulled out of going to the première. I wasn't friends with anyone on the film apart from one guy, so it doesn't surprise me they have been slagging off my acting. I don't claim to be the greatest actor in the world. It's a shame, but I don't have any hard feelings.'

Didn't he? That's not quite the way he was coming across. Alex was clearly a nice guy, albeit one who was becoming increasingly bemused by all the shenanigans surrounding him, but who could be surprised at that? Given the main complaint made about him since he'd become famous was that he was slightly on the vain side and not that he was a seriously unpleasant person, it was clear that Alex was an affable fellow, unprepared for all the vitriol. Jealousy played its part, of course, because he was also turning into a bona fide star.

Meanwhile, the critics too were had their say. 'This is the shoddiest excuse for a film I've seen in my life,' said *Heat Magazine*. 'Highlight, of course, is the Reidernator's much-vaunted sex scene, where he's channelling the passion and intensity of Beethoven (the giant St Bernard). The production values on *MILFs Like It Big* were much higher. That said, I reckon *Killer Bitch* has got a high chance of recouping its entire budget.'

At least the timing was good for someone – the film's makers.

Actually, not everyone hated it. Here is the *News of the World*: 'This is Grand Theft Auto meets I Spit on your Grave. A violent 21st-century British pantomime for the MTV generation. A middle finger in your face attitude. This is a must-see. This film is in a league of its own and has to be seen to be believed. You may read this review and think the film sounds vile, disgusting and morally depraved and you'd be wrong – you forgot to add bloody fantastic as well.'

Liam Galvin, writer and producer on *Killer Bitch*, knew exactly the effect he was out to create. 'What I want to do is give the public what they want: good-looking birds, big breasts, gangsters, guns and real fights,' he declared. 'You're really going to enjoy the film – we're not copping out.'

A selection of the very mixed reviews were as follows:

'A cult smash' – Channel 4.

'Sick and wrong. Made for distasteful and creepy twatbags, by distasteful and creepy twatbags' – 3am.co.uk.

'I guarantee that's a hit' – Michelle Heaton.

'Extreme violence and red-hot sex. A real lads' movie, a hardnosed gangster film which takes no prisoners' – *Sunday Sport*.

'It makes *You've Been Framed* look like *Apocalypse Now*!' – *Now Magazine*.

'Graphic sex scenes crackling with intensity' – the *People*.

'An intense, visceral viewing experience' – brutalashell.com.

'Ultra-violent gangster film' – the *Sun*.

'A sick movie... vile scenes... stomach-churning' – *Daily Mirror*.

'Exploitation film... modern horror' – *Irish Independent*.

'A violent gangster film' – *Daily Express*.

Liam Galvin, understandably, defended his movie. 'It's a gangster, crime and sensationalist film,' he said. 'It's about a game, where a woman has to kill five people or else her family and friends will be killed. Each person she has to kill takes her into a different fight scene, from cage fighting to boxing.'

And as for the notorious scene in the middle of the movie... There had been reports the couple were not acting, but actually having sex. Liam totally denied this. 'Yvette and Alex were just two actors filming a love scene,' he protested. 'They didn't have real sex and both were professional throughout. There's a real sex scene at the beginning – but it's not got Alex in it.'

Nor was it a rape scene. 'It was a love scene, not a rape scene,' Liam went on. 'The characters were just having rough sex. It was passionate, not rape. The film is heavy-duty and hard-hitting. There is another character who gets raped by a group of people, but Alex isn't involved in that at all.'

And Alex was, according to Liam, ideally cast. 'The reason we cast Alex was because it's very difficult to find someone who can act and fight,' he explained. 'Alex is very good-looking and rugged, and just looked fantastic. We got him before he was with his current partner, so he also had lots of charisma. I'm not saying he changed after he got together with Jordan, but his circumstances changed and he would come on set with loads of baggage. I think he found it hard to concentrate on the role because he had so much other stuff in his life.'

The last comment, of course, referred to the relationship that had just begun and it appeared that Katie had indeed taken a very active interest in proceedings when she discovered that her new man was making the film. 'I spoke to Katie – it was when Alex and her were abroad and she asked to speak to me,' Liam revealed. 'She was quite charming and just asked to see footage of the love scene between Alex and Yvette. I was fine with that, so sent it to them. I don't know what her reaction was, but after that Alex never returned.'

But there didn't appear to be many hard feelings. 'Alex was paid for the film, even though he didn't finish it,' said Liam. 'We are just a small company and even though we went over our budget and had to re-write and film loads more extra scenes after he pulled out, we aren't going to sue him. [But] I think it's a shame we haven't heard from him. We gave him an opportunity before he was famous and it would be nice if he acknowledged that.'

The film was never going to be a great classic but at least with all the resulting publicity, it was racing up the DVD charts. Executive producer John Fleming was also pretty pleased with the way it was working out. Who cared if the movie was garnering bad publicity? It was, at least, achieving publicity – which is what every film needs. 'If critics say it is the most appalling film ever made in the entire history of the world, then obviously that's good publicity,' John declared unabashed. 'If on the shelf it says this film is "vile and appalling" [then] people will pick it up and buy it. I don't mind if people say it's great, I don't mind if people say it is bad, but what I don't want is indifference. I worked as a researcher on populist programmes like *Tiswas*, *Game for a Laugh*, *Surprise, Surprise* and latterly, bizarre comedy programmes.

'I think *Killer Bitch* is populist entertainment sold to the widest possible market. It's not going to win a BAFTA, but it is very commercially made, maybe overly commercially made.'

But Alex now clearly wanted to distance himself from the whole furore. There had also been reports that he'd dropped his old crowd: all totally untrue. 'I read this week that some of my friends said I've dropped them,' he wrote plaintively. 'Of course I haven't. I don't see my mates as much as I'd like to, but I don't know where that story came from. Now I'm married, my wife is my first priority – but that doesn't mean my friends aren't important. Of course they are!'

Almost certainly, the rumour originated from people who were concerned about the amount of control that Katie was now exercising over Alex. Clearly she was the one setting the agenda: a nice guy like Alex didn't have a hope of standing up to her and there were real concerns about the effect this might have on his state of mind and career. Alex had been so completely subsumed into Katie's life that it was sometimes easy to forget that he'd had a life of his own before. If it all fell apart with Katie – and given the stories about rows, tensions, power struggles and the rest, it certainly didn't seem impossible –just what would he do next?

Meanwhile, Katie's old rival was fretting over worries of her own. Kerry was looking and feeling better than she had done in years but even so her single status was weighing heavily on her. She was beginning to feel very down in the dumps about finding a new man – and it wasn't about to be you-know-who, either.

'All talk of her and Peter Andre as an item is wide of the mark,' said a friend. 'He's supportive, but she's not really his type and he knows how fragile she is. She always ends up going for the wrong kind of man – she hates being alone. It's frustrating for her that there's no one on the scene when she's looking this good. She saw moving away from her old haunts and into her new Surrey mansion as the only way to make a clean break from all the bad influences and people who were jealous of her success. She did it for her career and for her kids but she feels like a fish out of water now. She doesn't have a great track record of being on her own for long so she's vulnerable to another risky relationship. She's insecure and needs a lot of reassurance. After Mark, it'll take a while for her to trust another man.'

Katie was watching proceedings with a decidedly jaundiced eye. Privately, she had become increasingly livid at the antics between Kerry and Pete: while it is unlikely that she thought there was anything in any of it, she was extremely unhappy that their names were so constantly linked. Remarks such as Kerry's artful, 'I've been round to Pete's house for tea with his family. He's been through a break-up too, so he's been great. He's my sweetheart and it's nice to know I'm not on my own,' had the effect of infuriating her all the more.

'It's bad enough Kerry being linked to Pete, but to say she wants to play happy families together is just adding insult to injury,' said a source close to Katie. 'Jordan was furious at Kerry saying she and Pete were planning an outing. She can't bear Kerry and doesn't want her to have anything to do with her kids.'

But Katie wasn't the only person that Kerry had been upsetting. In the death throes of her relationship with Mark, she'd attended a bootcamp and emerged looking far better than she had done in years – it was the start of her return to health and fitness. While there, she had met a fitness trainer called Kevin Green, a married father of three, and it was not long before a furious Mark was accusing her of having an affair. She wasn't, but she finally got round to admitting that something had happened between the two of them. 'I kissed him,' she said. 'There was no passion in it. There was a connection with Kev. I was physically attracted to him, but we were both married. I've never cheated and I thought, I can't be with somebody if I'm kissing someone else. He's married. It's completely wrong. I can only apologise for the upset I caused his wife. It was out of order, but we were both respectful and knew it could go no further.'

Unsurprisingly, Kevin's wife Sarah was not impressed. It hadn't gone any further than kissing, but even so, it was a line that should never have been crossed. 'Obviously it's upsetting,' she admitted, with some understatement. 'He's my husband. Being so public, it's hurtful and humiliating. I know what happened with Kerry and her ex, Brian, and I just think if someone has done that to you, you wouldn't do it to someone else so I find that difficult to understand.'

After she found out about the non-affair, Sarah went away for a couple of days. However, the couple had been together for a long time and nothing like this had ever happened before so after talking it through, they decided to give their relationship another go.

No serious damage was done to Kerry's reputation, probably because it hadn't gone very far and she'd had the wit to apologise. But watching this, Katie must again have been asking herself why the two celebrities were on the receiving end of such different attitudes from the public. Kerry, now revealed to have been involved in a flirtation with a married man, had once again got off scot-free, while the claws were out yet again for Katie.

Indeed, they were out to such an extent that one magazine did a round-up of all the rude things that other celebrities had said about Katie. 'Katie Price apparently said, "I don't want to be papped with that

Denise Welch,"' said actress Denise Welch. 'My son mocked, "Even Jordan doesn't want to be papped with you!" The shame!'

Then there was American model and actress Janice Dickinson: 'She's a rude bitch. Maybe she's just jealous because I did *Vogue* and she only did Page Three.'

And according to comedian Vic Reeves: 'Jordan was the rudest celebrity I ever met by a long way. We're all aware of her obnoxious character.'

Katie had certainly managed to ruffle a few feathers along the line. Even Alex Gerrard was dragged into it, not that she'd publicly slated anyone, but she and her footballer husband Steve had recently bumped into Kerry at Merseyside's Knowsley Safari Park and were pictured having a friendly chat. But Alex was supposed to have been a friend of Katie's – and everyone knew you couldn't hang out with both...

CHAPTER FIFTEEN

AN UNCERTAIN FUTURE

Katie and Alex continued to give out very mixed signals about the future of their relationship. They were spotted going to the Portland Clinic together, as keen as ever to have a child: there were rumours now that they were about to try fertility treatments. On the other hand, there were also reports that the arrangements for the blessing were being scaled back. Originally a big sit-down dinner had been on the cards, but now the couple had decided to have a buffet instead. But nothing interfered with business – whatever the status of the pregnancy, Katie was preparing to launch a new range of babywear at Birmingham's Baby Show.

Nothing deterred, Kerry was thought to have been

shopping for wedding dresses (actually, it was almost certainly an evening gown that she was looking for, but onlookers were nonetheless thrilled). Pete continued to be coy, hinting that he might be looking for a girlfriend, but that it wasn't going to be Kerry. But they were still good friends who were there for each other, because each knew exactly what the other was going through. Kerry's divorce proceedings went on, becoming nastier all the time.

Tit for tat continued on all sides. Was Kerry the new Katie? Was Alex the new Pete? Was Katie's star on the wane as Kerry's began to rise? (No.) Who would get the highest ratings on reality TV? And whatever one person had done, the others had to match, too. In 2009, Pete appeared at the Edinburgh Television Festival. Now, in 2010, Katie was about to do the same. 'She'll be the biggest attraction of the festival,' said a spokeswoman. 'She knows she'll have the ears of some of the most influential people in TV when she appears and she'll make the most of it.'

'Katie is a high-profile media figure who you can't ignore,' said a source. 'She knows full well she'll have the ears of some of the biggest movers and shakers in TV when she appears in Edinburgh – and she'll make the most of it.'

It was a war that showed no signs of abatting, but the real battle being waged was Katie Price against the world. Husbands came and went, friends passed through the drama, and the ever-changing cast list kept throwing up new participants with whom Katie could connect, but at the centre of it all was Katie herself. Brow ever more frozen, lurching from one over-the-top outfit to another, the fact is that whatever her detractors might say about her, Katie really is at the top of her game.

For Katie is unique. She is a glamour model gone mainstream, a woman who simply doesn't fit into any of the categories used to describe most celebrities today. Pete may have left her, but she is no victim and she would certainly never have allowed herself to be pushed around in the way that Kerry has been by Mark. She dominates her men and every situation she inhabits; she is a type of celebrity of the type never before seen in Britain.

And there is every indication that she will go on until she tires of it – which will be never. For Katie has had one supremely successful love affair, one that shows no sign of ending: it's love affair with the public – and it will run and run.